THE COMPLETE GUIDE TO

RENOVATING OLDER HOMES:

HOW TO MAKE IT EASY AND SAVE THOUSANDS

BY JEANNE B. LAWSON

THE COMPLETE GUIDE TO RENOVATING OLDER HOMES: HOW TO MAKE IT EASY AND SAVE THOUSANDS

Library of Congress Cataloging-in-Publication Data

Lawson, Jeanne B.
  The complete guide to renovating older homes : how to make it easy and save thousands / by Jeanne B. Lawson.
    p. cm.
Includes bibliographical references and index.
ISBN-13: 978-1-60138-242-9 (alk. paper)
ISBN-10: 1-60138-242-1 (alk. paper)
1. Dwellings--Remodeling. 2. Dwellings--Maintenance and repair. I. Title.

TH4816.L34 2010
643'.7--dc22
                            2010005317

Printed in the United States

PROJECT MANAGER: Kim Fulscher • kfulscher@atlantic-pub.com
PEER REVIEWER: Marilee Griffin • mgriffin@atlantic-pub.com
ASSISTANT EDITOR: Angela Pham • apham@atlantic-pub.com
INTERIOR DESIGN: Samantha Martin • smartin@atlantic-pub.com
FRONT & BACK COVER DESIGN: Jackie Miller • millerjackiej@gmail.com

Printed on Recycled Paper

TABLE OF CONTENTS

AUTHOR

ACKNOWLEDGMENTS

This book is sincerely dedicated to my father, who was the most talented home renovator I have ever met; and to my mother, who supported me in all of my adventures and career choices.

To my husband, Bob, who is my home renovation partner and provides inspiration and insight on all aspects of our life.

To Kim Fulscher and all others at Atlantic Publishing Group, Inc. who contributed to helping me write this book.

TRADEMARK
STATEMENT

We recently lost our beloved pet "Bear," who was not only our best and dearest friend but also the "Vice President of Sunshine" here at Atlantic Publishing. He did not receive a salary but worked tirelessly 24 hours a day to please his parents. Bear was a rescue dog that turned around and showered myself, my wife, Sherri, his grand-parents Jean, Bob, and Nancy, and every person and animal he met (maybe not rabbits) with friendship and love. He made a lot of people smile every day.

We wanted you to know that a portion of the profits of this book will be donated to The Humane Society of the United States. *–Douglas & Sherri Brown*

The human-animal bond is as old as human history. We cherish our animal companions for their unconditional affection and acceptance. We feel a thrill when we glimpse wild creatures in their natural habitat or in our own backyard.

Unfortunately, the human-animal bond has at times been weakened. Humans have exploited some animal species to the point of extinction.

The Humane Society of the United States makes a difference in the lives of animals here at home and worldwide. The HSUS is dedicated to creating a world where our relationship with animals is guided by compassion. We seek a truly humane society in which animals are respected for their intrinsic value, and where the human-animal bond is strong.

Want to help animals? We have plenty of suggestions. Adopt a pet from a local shelter, join The Humane Society and be a part of our work to help companion animals and wildlife. You will be funding our educational, legislative, investigative and outreach projects in the U.S. and across the globe.

Or perhaps you'd like to make a memorial donation in honor of a pet, friend or relative? You can through our Kindred Spirits program. And if you'd like to contribute in a more structured way, our Planned Giving Office has suggestions about estate planning, annuities, and even gifts of stock that avoid capital gains taxes.

Maybe you have land that you would like to preserve as a lasting habitat for wildlife. Our Wildlife Land Trust can help you. Perhaps the land you want to share is a backyard—that's enough. Our Urban Wildlife Sanctuary Program will show you how to create a habitat for your wild neighbors.

So you see, it's easy to help animals. And The HSUS is here to help.

THE HUMANE SOCIETY OF THE UNITED STATES.

2100 L Street NW • Washington, DC 20037 • 202-452-1100
www.hsus.org

Chapter 3: The Tools and Skills of the Trade **49**

Chapter 4: Get a Helping Hand, then Get a Start **77**

Chapter 5: Working Up from the Bottom **93**

Chapter 6: From the Top to Bottom and the Outside to the Inside **101**

FOREWORD

Renovating any home can be challenging, and working with an older home has developed a reputation for being especially so. With an older home, one might face issues with structural integrity, energy efficiency, outdated utilities, asbestos and other hazardous materials, and more. However, even with these challenges, renovating an older home can be incredibly worthwhile and rewarding. Whether captured by the charm of period craftsmanship, motivated to restore a historic gem, or simply attempting to update an older space to contemporary needs, more and more people today are turning to work with older structures.

With the challenges of an older home in mind, author Jeanne B. Lawson has crafted a wonderfully accessible and comprehensive guide for planning and achieving your remodeling goals — whatever the scope — while saving money and time. Whether you are a seasoned professional with many projects under your belt or someone who does not yet own a hammer, *The Complete Guide to Renovating Older Homes: How to Make it Easy And Save Thousands* is an important text to add to your reference collection.

The built environment is not static and unchanging, but multi-layered and ever growing. We cannot (and should not) deny innovation, new methods, new designs, additions, and alterations. But although we march forward, there is no reason for these renovations to be tackled without preservation of the old in mind. Many of us, whether we are aware of it or not, either live or work in surroundings dominated by buildings at least 50 years old. We have become heirs to a huge legacy of architecture of all shapes and sizes.

By choosing to renovate an older home, you have the opportunity to help protect the complex fabric of your built environment. You are also supporting the health of your city and our community. Furthermore, the renovation of a previously built home can have much less of an impact on the environment — and our wallet — than building an entirely new home from the ground up.

As someone trained in the field of historic preservation, and in the middle of my very own do-it-yourself renovation of a mid-century home, I found the information contained in Lawson's text to be enormously helpful, and I am thrilled to add it to my assortment of tools.

For those who are new to remodeling and older properties, this book will walk you through everything you need to know, from budgeting to materials, tool purchases, hiring contractors, historic preservation tax credits, and more. Lawson goes through several areas of the house and details how you can renovate each while retaining its original beauty. For those who are more experienced, this book will continue to serve as an invaluable reference guide that everyone in the field should not be without. Good luck!

EMILY BURROWS
Historian

INTRODUCTION

Have you noticed how many new homes mirror the styles of the past? The "new" farmhouse and the "new" bungalow are names given to architectural plans sold today. The number of homes that duplicate older styles indicates that many homeowners are attracted to and appreciate the designs of the older homes, but they do not want to tackle the challenges of rehabilitating an original.

On the other hand, there are many homeowners who want the challenge of bringing an old gem back to life. Fixing its flaws and enhancing its interior and exterior can make an older home a vital part of its community. The goal of this book is to provide practical information and insight into the anatomy of an older-home renovation project.

Everyone wants to save money, so offering cost-saving tips are a priority. Whether or not you decide to do all the work, some of the work, or none of the work, you will find advice on how to transform a home into a more functional and pleasing environment. This book is not about why some homeowners prefer an older house instead of a new house, or a contemporary style instead of Victorian — it is an instruction guide on the best practices for home renovation projects that increase its resale value and creates a more enjoyable living space for its occupants.

Creating the space of your dreams is a combination of inspiration and practicality. As we live in our homes, we figure out what is wrong with them. It will not take long to get tired of the vivid shag wall-to-wall carpeting in the master bedroom that looked fine when the house was bought. Nor will it take long to realize the dark paneling in the family room just does not go with contemporary furniture and flat screen television. Sharing one bathroom with your spouse was cozy when you first got married, but ten years of marriage and three children later, the coziness has turned into chaos. It is through time and frustration we figure out what changes would make our home a better place. Day dreaming, looking at magazines, watching home renovation television programs, and reading books like this one is time well spent to make those dreams come true. When it comes time to choose what needs renovating, repairing, tearing down, and building up, your practical knowledge will come in handy. Keep track of your ideas and begin to lay the foundation for your plans.

The year a home is built is the ultimate deciding factor as to whether a home is old or modern. Anything built after 1950 is considered a modern home. An older home can be modernized when it is renovated with the installation of new conveniences and efficient systems.

Renovating an older home can be time-consuming, expensive, nerve-racking, and a messy process full of challenges. This is especially true for a home that has been neglected or abandoned. Yet, there is something very fulfilling about the sense of achievement and satisfaction one feels when restoring a part of history. It is quite possible to take a 100-year-old home and make it modern with central heat and air conditioning systems, a new electrical wiring system and circuits, energy-efficient windows, new insulation, a kitchen with all of today's conveniences, and a spa bathroom.

The fact you are reading this book is positive proof that you have taken the leap to transform a house into a dream home. Researching and learning as much as possible about your older or historic house will be valuable. At a minimum, it is helpful to know the house's age, architectural style, and any history it might have in the community. If your house has some significance in the town, then there might be some old pictures of it in the community's archives.

Before making plans to renovate your home, it is essential to assess your home in its current condition. Take a look at the Home Inspection Evaluation Checklist in Appendix A of this book. Here, you can rate the different areas and parts of your home based on their condition. The scale ranges from excellent all the way to very poor, including an allotted space to record any necessary repair costs.

It does not matter whether the plan is to live in the home or sell it for a profit. No matter what the motivation is or how extensive your skill set, this book offers a complete guide to home renovations. The first few chapters of this book will present the steps and information needed prior to taking on the expense of renovating an older home. The more time invested up-front to plan for renovations, the less time spent later on regretting poorly thought-out decisions. The remainder of this book goes into more specific details on approaching and completing the work. So roll up your sleeves, get out a pencil and notebook, and learn how to transform a house into a unique space that exemplifies your personal style, ingenuity, and perspiration.

CHAPTER 1

Save Money in Your Renovations

Saving Money

Before beginning any specific how-to instructions, it is best to learn how to save money. These cost-saving tips will help save on home renovation projects starting at the beginning and help to stay within budget.

The essence of saving money comes down to two principles: 1) smart planning, and 2) the more you do yourself, the more money you will save. Depending on the project and skill level, you might have to hire professionals to complete all or some of the work. Smart planning comes in handy when figuring out that you will actually save money by hiring someone else to do the work. This statement might appear to contradict principle two, but there are times when it is better to hire a professional. Taking on a project that is beyond your expertise can result in a loss of time and money, so seeking the help of a professional is sometimes necessary. For those with minimal skills, there are still tasks that can be completed and that will help save money. If you do a good job, you can use the money you saved for another upgrade to better-quality building materials, or to buy some of those finishing touches to complete the project.

The reasons to renovate or restore a home vary from person to person. Maybe you have a problem in your home that needs to be fixed, or you do not like a particular feature. It could be that a system is no longer functioning properly and needs to be replaced or upgraded. Perhaps you have run out of space and want to add on an addition or change the floor plan. Another reason for improving your property is the desire to sell it. Having it in the best shape possible will enable you to market it at a higher list price.

No matter the reason, we first need to identify the desired result and then plan in advance the best approach to completing the work. If your motivation is to renovate to sell the house, then the more you save means more profit in your pocket. For example, when renovating the bathroom, do not buy designer fixtures. On the other hand, if the plan is to live in your house for many years, consider investing in top-of-the-line building materials.

Ways to Save on Your Project

Advance planning: The more you can plan, the more you can save

- **Turn to the experts** — For those do-it-yourselfers who know what they want, but need help putting their plan into focus, hire a designer or architect for a consultation session. These professionals bring experience, education, and perhaps more importantly, a fresh set of eyes to your project. They do not have to manage the renovation — they just have to supply concrete suggestions and creative insight. Have them prepare sketches and designs that can be incorporated into your plan of action.

- **As seen on television** — Home renovation television programs are a great way to gather ideas for your project. These programs provide a bird's eye view into other people's homes and problems.

- **Try to have professionals and contractors do their work during their off-peak times** — Prices will usually be lower when their schedules are not full, and there is a good chance your project will not run into delays.

- **Joint ventures** — Sometimes a contractor might be able to combine similar jobs and save on materials. If he or she has two jobs installing hardwood floors, then buying more wood flooring could yield cost savings to both clients.

- **Watch for sales** — Make purchases on supplies, materials, tools, and equipment when there is a clearance sale or a substantial discount. For example, if a store places a custom order and the customer returns it, the store is usually willing to sell this order at a reduced price. The retailer cannot usually return it to the manufacturer, so they are motivated to sell it for cost just to get rid of it. Most stores charge a re-stocking fee on custom orders. This means that if it is returned, then the original customer will have to pay this re-stocking fee. The store has been partially compensated for its effort and is still motivated to sell it at a discount.

- **Refrain from buying something just because it is on sale** — Certain sale purchases can lead to regret later. For instance, if a porcelain sink is what you really want, but you buy a stainless-steel sink because it is on sale — you might not be happy in the long run. It is better to spend more on the sink you want and be happy with it for years to come than to save a few dollars. There is a balancing act between saving money and happiness.

- **Buy display models** — Retail stores will periodically change out their display models and sell the older styles at a reduced price.

- **When the big home improvement stores bring in new styles, they reduce the prices on their existing inventory** — (But small retailers can offer some good deals, too.) Sometimes they need the room for new stock, so they will offer deals at an attractive price (make sure it is what you want).

- **The right time for the right project** — Plan projects in a sequence that makes sense. If you need a new roof, do that project before painting the house and installing new gutters. Do not take the chance of damaging new gutters or a paint job with the rough work that goes on while installing a new roof.

- **Talk the talk. Learn the home improvement language** — *See the Glossary of this book; it will help when working with contractors and subcontractors.* One of the best ways to communicate effectively with contractors and subcontractors is to know the home improvement language. Never be afraid to ask questions. A little knowledge might lead to learning about a valuable shortcut a professional does to save money.

Do the dirty work: Roll up your sleeves, break a sweat, and save

- **Do the demolition yourself** — Instead of paying a contractor to demolish the kitchen, invite family and friends to help. Be sure to dress appropriately. Wear safety glasses, work clothes and gloves, and thick-soled shoes or boots to prevent injuries. Your tetanus shots should be up to date, along with anyone helping with the project.

- **Clean up the work site** — Work out this detail up-front with the contractor. Many are amenable to helping clients save money; after all, contractors rely on referrals and references for new customers.

- **Work safe and smart at all times** — If you plan to tackle a project after you have returned home from work, make sure you are not too tired to use power tools.

- **Do the prep work** — Before the contractor or subcontractor comes in to do their work, get some tasks completed so they can get right to work. This can include removing the carpeting and linoleum, prepping walls for painting, or cleaning walls, woodwork, or floors. These details can be negotiated in the contract.

Do some heavy work

Do the legwork for your own projects and for the contractor. Remember, time is money, and the more work you do for the project, the more you keep expenses down.

- **When possible, pick up your own materials** — This will save on delivery fees and the cost of sending the contractor or subcontractor to pick up materials. When materials or equipment must be delivered, try to negotiate a reduced rate.

- **Have a suitable vehicle** — Do not ruin a nice truck or car hauling materials and trash. It might be worth buying or renting a pickup truck or van, depending on the size of the renovation. Another good investment is a trailer. Trailers are ideal for moving equipment and for hauling material or debris. Make sure the trailer is large enough to haul 4- by 8-foot sheets of plywood and other large items. If you choose a trailer with a wooden deck instead of steel, be sure to get pressure-treated wood. This is better because pressure-treated wood is treated with preservatives that resist rot and insects.

- **Check your state's registration and insurance requirements before making a purchase or a rental** — This information can be obtained at a local registry or division of motor vehicles. To find a local registry office, log onto the Unofficial DMV Guide's Web site at **www.dmv.org**. Backing up a vehicle is a little tricky with a trailer attached, so be sure to get some help and practice.

- **Do your own shopping** — Be sure to get specifications and sizes from the contractor, if they are doing the work. If you are doing the work, remember the Italian proverb "measure twice and cut once." This advice goes for all measurements. For those who wear reading glasses, it is best to put them on for measuring.

- **Apply for your own permits when possible** — The time it takes to obtain these may differ, depending on the type of permit needed and which state it is being applied for in. This will save money by not paying someone else to do it. Plus, if there is a problem with a contractor, you will have control over the project through the permits. Some states require a signature by the homeowner for all permits, so it might save time to apply for them. For some projects and renovations, the contractors must apply for the permit, in order to prove they have the license and insurance to do the work.

Other tips for saving

- **Buy used materials** — In some cases, used might be best because the cost savings can be substantial. Trying to find original fixtures, trims, and molding for an older home can be a challenge, but there are places to start your search. Try the Craigslist Web site at **www. craigslist.org** to find raw materials and other items for free or at a reduced price. Find the state and the closest major city to your home and start to see what is available. Check the Web site often because new listings are added daily.

- **Auctions, yard sales, salvage yards, and antique shops** — These are other resources to check out when in need of architectural elements, fixtures, and building materials.

- **Habitat for Humanity has a retail resource called a ReStore** — This is a good place to find original building materials and tools. *See "Habitat for Humanity ReStore" in Chapter 3.*

- **One caveat when purchasing original building materials is they might not work or fit** — Try to make sure they are in working order. For example, old plumbing materials might not be cost-efficient if they do not work or require major repairs. If something is a great price but does not work, then you will have to buy a replacement.

- **Locate businesses that sell antique reproductions** — There are companies such as Renovator's Supply that sell hard-to-find reproductions of antique hardware and architectural elements. Their Web site is **www.rensup.com**.

Restoration Hardware is a retail and online source for hardware, fixtures, and other building elements that are classic and might fit into the décor of an older home. The Web site is **www.restorationhardware.com/rh/index.jsp**, but they have actual retail locations in the United States and Canada. The Web site, **www.oldhouses.com**, is for anyone who loves old houses. The site offers a comprehensive list of old and historic house restoration supplies and services, plus a list of old homes for sale. A direct link to this resource is **www.oldhouses.com/old-house-suppliers-services.htm#suppliers**.

- **Do not be shy about asking for a deal** — If you plan to purchase materials and supplies, plumbing, and light fixtures from one or two home building centers, ask for a builder's discount. General contractors might be eligible for at least a 10 percent discount (or more) on purchases. Some retail stores are willing to give a discount on a large order, whether it is a custom order or merchandise right off the shelf. Keep in mind many retail clerks do not have the authority to approve discounts, so ask for the store manger or sales manager in advance. Discounts are a good way to keep customers coming back for materials and supplies.

- **When making online purchases, ask for a discount on materials, supplies, and tools** — If the contractor has a discount with a particular supplier, ask if you can utilize it when making purchases on a project that they are working on.

Hiring Professionals versus Do-it-yourself

For anyone who wants to save money on projects, keep this advice in mind: The more work you do yourself, the more money you will save, as long as the work is completed close to a professional's standard. Work with someone who has skills that complement your own.

Local building codes dictate when the services of a professional is required. Do your research, and take time to familiarize yourself with the permit laws in your state, city, or town. To find building codes for a specific state, use a universal Web address (you will need to insert the two-letter state abbreviation). For example, this is the Web site for California: **www.state.ca.us**. Once in the state's Web site, use the search feature and type in "building codes." California's Web site has a "Home & Family" tab, and from there you can choose "Housing."

Every homeowner renovator should take an honest assessment of their own abilities and the skills needed to complete the project. If you do not have what it takes to get the project done on your own, call in a professional.

Roles of a general contractor, subcontractor, or professional

Depending on the size of the project, it might be best to hire a general contractor, subcontractor, or professional to complete some or all of the renovation work. The keys to managing a successful renovation project are the same as with other projects: Understand the scope and purpose of the job, stay in contact with the professional doing the work, develop a positive relationship with those working on the project, and communicate on a regular basis.

General contractors

A general contractor manages the entire project by coordinating and supervising the work at the construction site from the preliminary development stage until the work is completed. Some general contractors take on different kinds of work, but most specialize in one type and size project.

General contractors provide a quote to the homeowner after they have reviewed the project plans and specifications. The quote is based on material, labor, and safety considerations. Other duties of the general contractor include:

- Hires subcontractors
- Sets work schedules
- Handles payroll
- Manages the quality of the project work
- Provides the equipment for the job
- Orders the supplies (such as concrete, steel, electrical equipment, and lumber) and arranges for the delivery of equipment and supplies
- Applies for and manages all permits and licenses
- Follows all building codes and safety regulations mandated by the city or town and the state governmental entities
- Oversees project expenditures
- Assumes the risks and responsibilities in making sure the project is done according to the contract

When hiring a general contractor, turn the entire project over to him or her, unless the contract states that the homeowner will handle certain aspects of the project.

CASE STUDY: A GENERAL CONTRACTOR'S ADVICE

Barbara Taylor
General Contractor and Consultant
Green Sea, South Carolina
sommerbys@aol.com

"There are different degrees of historic restorations that can be completed on a home and restoring an older or historic home is not for everyone," Barbara Taylor said. "The degrees range from historic purist, who will only replace with original parts, to the individual who can be completely satisfied with using historic reproduction replacement parts when completing a renovation project."

In the last 30 years as a general contractor, Taylor has been involved in dozens of renovations of both older and historic homes. Any person considering these types of renovations "needs to have passion, a love for an historic house, and a good-sized checkbook to take on restoring an historic house," Taylor said. "This is not for your average homeowner because the work is intricate and takes a long time to complete."

There are many challenges to restoring an historic home. Some of the main ones include:

- The foundation
- The plumbing system
- The electrical system
- The location of original replacement parts

The foundation

"Before purchasing an older home or doing any work on it, the first thing to consider is the state of the foundation. This is a big challenge because if the foundation is in poor shape, this will influence every other aspect of the house," Taylor said. Before builders apply the concrete onto footings and slab foundations, stone is used to support the home. Once these components crumble, the house settles. With walls compressing due to settling, Taylor said certain foundations cannot be repaired. "Even though a contractor might want to jack the house to repair the damaged foundation, he runs the risk of damaging other parts of the house," Taylor said. "The windows, ceilings, and walls can crack, and this impacts every room in the house." In the case that the home rests on rotted wood, everything is thrown out of proportion, and all rooms are thrown out of alignment.

Most historic and older homes have plaster on the walls. The home-owner must decide if it will be necessary to repair the plaster or replace it with Sheetrock™. This will depend on personal preference and the condition of the walls.

"Plaster does not always have the smooth and perfect flat look that Sheet-rock will have," Taylor said. "Even though plaster has its imperfections, it looks more authentic in an older home." Plaster replicates the look of old Tuscany walls and creates a Venetian finish. This is a costly design for walls, running about $50 per square foot. So, for a 9- by 12-foot room, the finishing expense will be $3,000.

The plumbing system

Most historic or older homes will have old cast-iron pipes. PVC will not connect to the cast iron. Trying to repair cast iron in an older home is very difficult because many of the fittings will be rusted and tough to remove without breaking. It is best to replace all the plumbing with new instead of trying to repair them. Taylor's advice is to use new cast-iron pipes or convert everything to PVC.

The electrical system

It is wise to have a licensed electrician, experienced in working on older homes, evaluate the current system and bring the house up to code. This is a good investment for both the safety of the occupants and the enjoyment of modern comforts.

Finding replacement parts

Another big challenge in being a purist is hunting down architectural elements like windows and doors, fixtures, hardware, and other replace-ments parts. The best places to look for these items are yard sales, flea markets, antique stores, and through Internet searches. Most of the challenges can be overcome by writing a check, but this is not the case when it comes to finding original replacement parts. "If they don't readily exist, it can wind up taking ten years to find them," Taylor said.

Do-it-yourself general contractors

Some homeowners might decide to be their own general contractor, which means they will handle everything from evaluating the project, estimating the costs, hiring the subcontractors, arranging for the permits, ordering all the materials and equipment, and overseeing all aspects of the project to completion. This is a viable option for those who have the time and expertise. For some projects it might be best to hire a subcontractor, which saves time and money in the long run. Other benefits to doing the work yourself are that you can buy some of the materials at wholesale; the work can be done at your convenience; and only one project takes priority — your house. Expect to save about 30 percent if you become the general contractor.

Subcontractors

Some jobs might require the services of a subcontractor, or "subbing out." This means hiring a subcontractor to do the work. Using a subcontractor is a good idea if the project is large, or if you need a skilled tradesperson to do the work. The types of work you might hire a subcontractor for are painting, carpentry, plumbing, electrical, drywall, tiling, carpet installation, masonry, foundation work, roofing, window replacement, and floor refinishing. This is not an exhaustive list, but this is a general idea of the types of help needed.

Professionals

The size and scope of a project will dictate the need to hire a professional such as an architect to draw up plans and blueprints; an interior designer to create a vision for the space; an engineer to resolve a structural problem; or an attorney to read over a contract.

An architect can manage the complete renovation project or can evaluate and consult on the structure and enhancements and changes planned. An architect or civil engineer can help with a major remodeling project by providing blueprints and specifications for the work to be done.

An engineer offers advice on the structural and system aspects of a home. Along with the architect, an engineer can inform the homeowner about the structural, mechanical, electrical, plumbing, foundation, framework, and exterior implications, as well as the potential hazards of making major changes to the home. The degree of their involvement depends on the homeowner's desire for help.

CASE STUDY: ONE INTERIOR DESIGNER'S UNIQUE APPROACH

Sarah Barnard
Los Angeles, California
www.sarahbarnard.com
(310) 823-7331

Sarah Barnard is an interior designer who works with homeowners to craft gracious interiors that reflect the unique qualities of each older home and architectural site being renovated. Her approach is to salvage as many unique architectural features of the home as possible in order to maintain the distinctive character of the property. When contacted by a homeowner or professional, Barnard begins the process of helping her clients by following the steps below:

1. Meet with homeowners to ascertain goals
2. Assess the architecture of the property
3. Prepare an inventory of items to salvage and items to replace
4. Draft plans for the renovation and prepare a list of materials needed
5. Assist homeowner in selecting qualified craftsmen
6. Act as the owner's ally throughout the renovation process

Barnard will ask the homeowner many questions to assess the existing architecture of the property. Each home is unique, but below are some of the questions asked:

- What year was the property constructed?
- When were any renovations performed? To what extent were they completed?
- Are the paint colors true to the period of the house?

- Has the property been modified from its original design?
- Have the floors been changed or covered with carpet?
- Have the doors, windows, or lighting fixtures been changed?
- Has natural wood trim been painted?
- Has wrought iron been added to windows?
- Has the kitchen been changed to include modern fixtures?
- Has the bath been changed to include modern fixtures?
- Has paneling been placed on or removed from the walls?
- Has the ceiling been sprayed with acoustics?
- Have the interior doors been changed to slab hollow with modern door handles?
- Have the base and casing been replaced with a modern style (baseboards 8 inches tall changed to a 3.5 inches; or a casing 4.25 inches changed to 2.25 inches)?

Barnard offers these tips for homeowners prior to beginning interior and exterior projects with wood trim: "If the outside of the house has a stucco finish flush with the wood window trim, the chances are good that the wood siding is underneath," she said. "In most instances, stucco was placed right over the siding, and if the siding is in good condition, it can be refurbished back to its original charm."

Other factors to consider during the assessment of the property include:

- Look for signs of original wood trim when removing paneling, wall-paper, or drywall (nail holes and colored lines might indicate where the trim was originally located)
- Check under acoustic ceilings for original electrical boxes (indications of former overhead lights)
- Look behind wallpaper or paneling (former locations for sconces or wall lights)

When it comes to wood flooring, it should be reconditioned, not replaced.

Finally, Barnard said, "Do not replace wood windows. This will disqualify a house for the Mills Act, a program in which the homeowner might receive a reduction in property tax (10 to 50 percent) for agreeing to maintain the original characteristics of the home." Vinyl fencing is not permitted, as it may also lead to disqualification. More original components are desired as opposed to modernized counterparts.

The following are a few of Barnard's projects:

1912 arts and crafts home

The clients did most of the work and found hidden windows and a hidden fireplace behind 1970s siding. This house was the childhood home of Louis Zamperini, a war hero and Olympian. The homeowners formed a personal relationship with Zamperini and through family photographs were able to achieve high levels of accuracy in their restoration.

1927 Spanish eclectic home

Interior plaster was removed in a restorative effort and, to the owner's surprise, the ceiling collapsed. What started out as a project to renovate the kitchen, replace windows, and repair/replace plaster and stucco turned out to be the renovation of a whole house. This included replacing two fireplace facades, renovating an existing bathroom, and turning a coat closet into an extra bathroom.

How to Hire

Word-of-mouth is a good way to find a general contractor, subcontractor, or professional. Conducting the research before making a hiring decision saves time and money in the long run. This might seem tedious, but there is nothing worse than a failed renovation project. If the house being renovating is for sale, then there is greater pressure to finish the project on time and budget so it can be quickly put on the market. The following are steps to follow to find the best person (or company) to complete the project:

- **Request quotes from two to four individuals or companies —** Initial conversations on the telephone are fine, but it is imperative to meet potential candidates in person. A gut reaction can indicate how well the person is suited for the job. In some instances, you will be meeting with a company's sales representative and not the person actually doing the work. Be sure to ask to meet with the foreman who will be at the home on a daily basis.

- **If any professional, such as an electrician or plumber, needs to be licensed, ask to see their license** — Check to see if it is current and if it is the proper license for the work you need done. Some states will allow consumers to search their department of public safety database to determine if a professional's license is current. If this information is not readily available on a state's Web site, contact the city or town's building inspector for assistance.

- **Determine insurance coverage and if the professional is bonded.**

- **Find out if the professional has any infractions reported to local governing bodies or complaints against him or her with the Better Business Bureau (BBB)** — To find the BBB in your area, visit **www.bbb.org** and type in a ZIP code.

- **Ask for references, and really check them out.**

- **If possible, try to see work completed by the professional** — Try to visit a work site and see who is actually doing the job and their work habits. A messy job site and sloppy work will give a clear picture of what to expect at your home.

- **Always have a written contract. Take time to read and understand it** — Have an attorney read the contract prior to signing it, based on the total amount due to the contractor. For instance, if the project costs more than $25,000, then have an attorney read it over. The legal fee paid is well worth it. Make sure you clearly understand implications, stipulations, ramifications, and provisions if problems arise.

Questions to ask a contractor

Most professionals are willing to discuss their previous work. The following is a set of questions to ask to help make a decision:

- How long have you been in business?
- Do you have repeat clients, and what percentage of your business do they make up?
- Are you licensed?
- Are you insured?
- Are you bonded? If so, for how much?
- Is your work guaranteed or carrying a warranty? If yes, please provide details.
- How does pricing work, and when is payment due?
- Am I able to make changes mid-project? What is the procedure to do so?
- Do you have safety requirements on the job site for workers?
- What are your policies on job site cleanup?
- How many people will you have on the job at any time?
- What is the best way for us to communicate: e-mail, telephone, or at the job site?
- Who is my major point of contact within your business?
- How many projects do you have going on at any given time?
- Are there local projects or job sites I can view/visit?
- Do you specialize in any green building techniques? If so, what are they?
- Why should I hire you instead of a competitor?

Questions to ask a reference

Before hiring a contractor, do a reference check. Ask as many people as possible about the quality of a contractor's work as well as their business practices. Here is a set of questions to ask:

- What kind of project did you have done?
- Was the project completed successfully?
- What did you like about this contractor?
- What did you not like about this contractor?
- Were there any problems during the course of the project?
- If yes, how were these problems resolved?
- Were there open lines of communication?
- How long did the project take?
- Did all the work go according to schedule?
- Did all the work go according to budget?
- Did you have to move out during the renovations?
- How was your family accommodated during the renovations?
- Did any management changes take place during your project with the contractor? If yes, did they affect your project?
- Were you privy to any guarantees or warranties?

CHAPTER 2

Following the Rules

Promoting Health and Safety: Regulations, Codes, Permits, and Inspections

The state building codes

It is your responsibility to adhere to the building codes set forth by the city or town where the property is located. Each state creates building codes and requires homeowners to apply for a construction permit to ensure all new work — which includes repairs to older homes and new construction — meets minimum standards of safety. The standards protect any occupants of the property, those who have property adjacent to yours, and emergency response personnel responding to a potential problem at the home. The building codes will protect the property by promoting a safe and secure environment through the use of sound construction practices.

For example, the building codes in some communities require a shut-off to the electrical service located on the outside of the house. If there is a fire or flood at the home, the emergency personnel can quickly shut off the electricity to the house safely from the outside instead of going into the house to locate the electrical service box. Code inspectors will visit your property periodically to make sure the work is proceeding properly, or will at least visit at the end of the project to approve the work.

All states have building codes, and each local community will have its own system of enforcing them. It is up to you to learn which codes are pertinent to your projects. Most professionals, such as plumbers and electricians, are knowledgeable about local building codes. They will apply for the permits and are required to present their license and insurance documents to local authorities to prove their credibility.

Each state sets its own building codes, which all construction work and workers must adhere to. It is based on regional specifications, geology, and weather. For instance, building codes in the San Andreas Fault Line area of California will be different from those in the state of Florida, where hurricanes present a greater threat. Reed Construction Data, Inc. compiled a list of each state and their unique building codes. The site offers information on several cities and municipalities within each state. Visit the Web site at **www.reedconstructiondata.com/building-codes** to research your state's codes, link to your state's building code Web page, and obtain information on project leads and construction news.

Obtain the necessary permits before beginning work on the site. Historic annual building permit information is available at **www.census.gov/const/ www/permitsindex.html**. Click on "Permits by State" to research your state-specific permits. If you have a general contractor, he or she will usually pull the permits for you, or you might apply for them yourself. In most cases, the homeowner needs to sign the permit. Most communities have a Building Department where residents are able to find out how to obtain permits. There is usually a fee that needs to be paid for the permit. Some communities will charge a fee according to a proposed percentage of total construction costs, or building departments will have a set fee for a permit. Keep track of all permits and receipts.

A plot or design plan might be required in order to get the permit(s). All local buildings must abide by the code enforced by officials. Once you obtain permits, the government inspectors are aware of your project and will inspect the site and the work, usually when the homeowner or contractor requests an appointment. Although the code official is sometimes seen as an adversary, the inspector's mandate is to protect people and property. Inspectors will need to sign off and approve the work at a home after a permit is requested. If you are doing some ordinary cosmetic repairs, such as replacing the carpeting, refinishing hardwood floors, painting, wallpapering, or setting up swing sets, you will not have to apply for a permit.

Here are projects that will require a permit:

- Constructing a new home
- Adding an addition to the home
- Repairing, renovating, or installing new materials
- Changing the use of the property
- Demolishing existing structures
- Adding certificates of occupancy
- Installing a fire suppression system
- Altering or installing an exit from the home
- Installing a new electrical service or repairing an existing service
- Installing or repairing plumbing fixtures/systems
- Installing or repairing gas fixtures, appliances, or systems
- Installing heating, ventilation, and air conditioning systems

Some building department personnel are also involved in regulating the licenses and certification of construction and trade professionals. They might determine the criteria and safety for structural loads, foundations, and structural design.

Promoting health and safety

There are potential health concerns every homeowner needs to become aware of, especially if the home is an older one. The main ones are:

- Asbestos
- Radon
- Lead (in water or paint)

The Environmental Protection Agency (EPA) is the foremost federal agency involved in educating and protecting individuals from the impact of environmental factors that can have an impact on the safety and health of citizens. The EPA has regional offices throughout the country that are responsible for executing the EPA's national programs locally.

Asbestos

Asbestos is a mineral fiber that was once added to products as a strengthening agent and to provide heat insulation and fire resistance. Inhaling and being around high levels of asbestos fibers has been associated with illnesses such as lung cancer and mesothelioma, a cancer that forms in the chest lining and the abdominal cavity. Asbestosis may also develop, which is a chronic inflammatory condition of the lungs.

Where asbestos materials might be present in a home

The following are some of the common materials where asbestos might be found in a home:

- Shingles in the roofing and siding that are made of asbestos cement.
- Insulation in houses built between 1930 and 1950.

- Insulation in attic and walls made using vermiculite ore.
- Textured paints and patching compounds used on wall and ceiling joints prior to 1977.
- Artificial ashes and embers used in gas-powered fireplaces.
- Stovetop pads that were once made of asbestos and were used as a safe surface to place hot pots and pans to prevent burning or damaging surfaces. It is similar to a trivet.
- Old ironing board covers.
- The hearths, walls, and floors protecting wood-burning stoves, which might contain asbestos paper, millboard, or cement sheets.
- Vinyl floor tiles, the backing on vinyl sheet flooring, and their adhesives.
- The hot water and steam pipes, which might be covered with an asbestos insulation.
- Oil and coal furnaces and door gaskets.

To see a complete list of materials potentially containing asbestos, visit the EPA's Web site offering additional items at **www.epa.gov/earth1r6/ 6pd/asbestos.**

Determining if a material contains asbestos

The following are ways to determine if a material in the home definitely contains asbestos:

1. Check to see if the manufacturer's label is still on the item and if it states there is asbestos material on the product.

2. You can hire a professional to inspect the home for asbestos. His experience will alert him to typical asbestos-prone materials like heating pipes and furnaces.

3. Have an analysis of the material completed to determine if it contains asbestos. Some materials can be tested with either the polar-

ized light microscopy (PLM) or the transmission electron microscopy (TEM) testing equipment. Have a professional take samples and have the materials tested at an asbestos testing lab. It is best to only test damaged materials or materials that will be disturbed during a renovation project. If asbestos is in good condition, leave it alone. It will only hurt people if it is damaged or disturbed. Asbestos dust is harmful when it gets into the air, and this typically happens when it is damaged, moved, or removed.

What to do with asbestos in the home

If you know there is asbestos in your house and the affected area is not decaying, then the best course of action is to do nothing. Naturally occurring asbestos (NOA) is found in rocks and soil, so we are exposed to small quantities of asbestos each day. Geologists, engineers, environmentalists, and construction professionals help control the conditions that limit the potential harm from an NOA.

The problem occurs when asbestos-containing materials are disturbed and damaged. This can happen in a natural setting and in a home. Disturbing or damaging asbestos can result in crumbling asbestos fibers. If the fibers fall apart, they can turn into a powder. This is dangerous and can lead to a health hazard when inhaled. Keeping the asbestos materials in good condition is the best approach.

According to the EPA, if you see damaged asbestos or you are suspicious there might be a problem, hire a professional trained to work with asbestos to evaluate and analyze the situation. If there is a problem, there are two options to resolve the matter — repair or removal:

1. **Repair** — This method either seals or covers the asbestos material. Sealing (encapsulation) treats the material so the fibers are not released into the environment. Typically, pipes, furnaces, and boilers are removed with this technique. Sealing can cover the

asbestos with a paint-like product that penetrates and seals harmful fibers from being released. There are also spray-type adhesives that bind the asbestos fibers together. They are sprayed on wet, and when they dry, they form a hard seal over the asbestos. There is another form of repair that covers the asbestos with a wrap or insulation-type product. Exposed pipe's insulation can be covered with a protective wrapping material, and wraps can be cut to size or come in pre-shaped forms. There are shrink-wrap plastic products that cover the asbestos, too. Repairing the problem is usually cheaper than removal, but it might just be a temporary fix if the condition of the material changes or if the area where the asbestos is located is disturbed.

2. **Removal, also known as abatement** — This is the more expensive solution and, unless your local or state regulation requires it, this method should be considered the last option. The physical act of removing asbestos from the home creates the greatest risk of releasing the asbestos fibers. If asbestos could be disturbed during renovations, then removal may be the best option. Removal of asbestos is complex, so leave it to professionals with the proper training and credentials. Even the most minor of repair or removal project can be hazardous for those not properly trained or protected from the harms of asbestos fibers.

Hiring an asbestos professional

The federal government requires that individuals working with asbestos take and pass training courses. Some states might require other training in addition to the federal training requirements. The EPA provides each state's guidelines on training requirements. Once the coursework is completed, an application is submitted and, if approved, the individual will receive a certificate of accreditation. After the initial training is completed, the asbestos control professionals are required to take an annual refresher course. The requirements of taking the refresher courses for asbestos workers, from least skilled to most skilled, are:

- Asbestos worker (required)
- Asbestos supervisor (required)
- Asbestos contractor (required)
- Asbestos inspector (required)
- Management planner (required)
- Project designer (required)
- Project monitor (recommended)

It is advisable to hire one company to inspect the property, analyze the situation and, if necessary, propose a corrective course of action. Get at least three estimates for any asbestos project and check the credentials, training, and certificates of those who will perform the work.

There are ten regional offices in the United States, and these offices act in cooperation with federal, state, and local governments, academic institutions, and the private industry to help meet the needs of the individual states. To locate a regional office, visit the EPA's asbestos section on their Web site at **www.epa.gov/asbestos/pubs/regioncontact.html#State**. Some regional offices have lists of certified contractors.

Radon

Radon is known to be a cancer-causing radioactive gas that can be found in homes across the United States. These radioactive particles adhere to tissues of the lungs and can change the cell nature, which increases the risk of cancer. The National Cancer Institute states that cigarette smoking is the leading cause of cancer, followed by radon. According to the EPA in 2003, radon exposure causes approximately 21,000 lung cancer deaths per year, and 2,900 of these impact non-smokers. Furthermore, the report states that radon is the leading cause of lung cancer for non-smokers. To read more about the health implications of radon, visit both the National Cancer Institute's Web site at **www.cancer.gov/cancertopics/factsheet/Risk/radon** and the EPA's radon Web page at **www.epa.gov/radon/healthrisks.html**.

It is difficult to detect radon gas because we cannot see or smell it. Radon occurs when soil, rocks, and water contain a physical decay of uranium. Through this natural process, the uranium breaks down, and radon gets into the air. You could breathe in radon and not realize it. Both old and new homes can have problems with radon because it seeps through cracks in the foundation, cracks in solid floors, construction joints, cracks in walls, gaps in suspended floors and around service pipes, cavities inside walls, and through the water supply (wells).

There are many ways to test for radon in your home on your own. These affordable radon test kits can be purchased online and shipped directly to your home, and are also available at local hardware or home improvement stores. A good place to begin to learn about radon is the EPA's Web site and reading "A Citizen's Guide to Radon: The Guide to Protecting Yourself and Your Family From Radon" at **www.epa.gov/radon/pubs/citguide.html**.

To locate your state radon council, visit their Web site at **www.epa.gov/iaq/whereyoulive.html**. Once you find your state's office, they can provide radon information specific to your state, and a list of licensed or certified technicians. Some state programs offer free or low-cost kits. If you decide to hire a professional, make sure his or her license is valid, and get estimates before making a decision. Also, determine if a test is required as a condition of the sale when you are buying or selling a home.

The amount of radon in the air is measured in "picocuries per liter of air," or pCi/L. After testing, if your house has elevated radon levels — four picocuries per liter (pCi/L) or higher — there are practical solutions to resolve the problem. The solution will be based on the design and construction of your home, and a professional radon contractor can present the best options. There are no known methods to eradicate radon from your home, but there are ways to lower the levels. If you conduct a self-test and it proves positive for radon, then have a trained radon contractor inspect and re-test the home to determine specific radon levels again; let them offer solutions.

The most common and effective solution to fixing a radon problem is the vent pipe system and fan. The radon is moved from underneath the house, and the system then disperses it outside. Another name for this is a soil-suction radon reduction system. Similar systems are available if the house has a crawl space. This method will not require major changes to the home; however, if you have foundation cracks or other openings, it is wise to repair them or block them off so the radon will not make its way back into the home.

A heat-recovery ventilator (HRV), or air-to-air heat exchanger, improves ventilation while lessening the levels of radon inside the home when installed. Although the HRV is more efficient in reducing radon levels when used solely in basements, it has the capability to ventilate all or most of a home by using heated or cooled air to warm or cool air flowing in.

Lead in the Home

Lead in the home can pose a health risk. It is a toxic metal that was once an ingredient commonly put into everyday products like plumbing materials and paint. These lead-based products can create health problems in children and adults. For anyone planning to renovate or build a home, it is important that they become knowledgeable about the environmental impact their work site will have on the neighborhood. Get familiar with the EPA's programs and mandates regarding lead to make certain you are not breaking any of their laws or codes.

Lead in water

Lead is a metal commonly used in household plumbing materials and municipal water service lines. It is unusual to find lead in the original water source coming from a municipality, but the risks are higher in the home when tap water travels through corroded water pipes. Children who are 6 years old and younger are the most vulnerable population. Lead poisoning can be manifested in problems with physical and mental developmental, behavioral problems, learning disabilities, seizures, and even death. Adults exposed to lead contaminants have higher blood pressure levels and can develop kidney problems.

Homes built prior to 1986 are more likely to have lead pipes, fixtures, and lead solder. The new and legal "lead-free" plumbing materials can be composed of at least 8 percent lead. The brass or chrome-plated brass faucets and fixtures are cause for concern; note that lead is more likely to turn up in hot water instead of cold water.

Lead in paint

In the past, lead had been used as an ingredient to manufacture many products — paint being one such product. Exposure to lead-based paint can lead to adverse health problems. Once a structure that has lead paint is cut, demolished, or sanded, toxic paint chips become airborne. Ingesting or breathing in these particles can be a health hazard to all ages. Lead paint in older homes needs to be treated in a safe and cautious manner, especially during a renovation project.

If a house was built before 1978 and the paint is chipping, peeling, or showing wear, the EPA suggests that parents test children living in the home to determine if there is a high level of lead in their blood. Homeowners should consider getting their house tested. There are home tests, but they have not proved to be as reliable and accurate as when a professional conducts the test. There are two options available when it comes to testing:

1. A paint inspection will reveal the lead content of every different type of painted surface in the home, but it will not tell whether the paint is a hazard. Neither will it tell how to resolve the problem if there are some surfaces painted with lead.

2. A risk assessment will determine if there are any sources of serious lead exposure and will offer the best course of action to resolve these potential hazards.

Tips to remove lead-based paint from the home

Here are suggestions on how to remove or make safe lead paint in the home:

- If possible, completely remove the lead-painted item from the home.

- A short-term, interim solution is to spray the painted surface with a sealant or repaint the surface. Keep in mind that sealants and paints wear out, chip, and peel, exposing the lead paint again.

- If there are small areas that have been painted with lead paint, strip the area by using a wet chemical stripper, then use a paint scraper to remove the residual paint.

- Avoid sanding or grinding to eliminate lead paint dust. If you are using a sander, be sure it is shrouded (a dust containment system to contain the dust) and the equipment is attached to a HEAP filter.

- If a heat gun is used to remove paint, make certain it is no hotter than 11 degrees Fahrenheit.

- If the area that has lead paint is large and involves removing walls or a Sheetrock section, then preventing the dust is critical. One solution is to cover old Sheetrock with new Sheetrock. If only half the wall needs replacing, affix the wainscoting to the bottom half of a potential danger spot.

- If you need to remove lead paint from the whole house, consider hiring professionals experienced in this type of work. The key is to prevent exposure to the lead dust as the paint is being removed.

The EPA has numerous brochures and how-to suggestions on how to safely remove lead paint from homes. To read more about lead paint and suggestions on ways to resolve the problem, visit the EPA's Web site link offering practical solutions at **www.epa.gov/lead/pubs/howto.htm**. The EPA, in conjunction with Housing and Urban Development (HUD), the Centers for Disease Control and Prevention (CDC), and the Occupational Safety and Health Administration (OSHA), have created a comprehensive field guide with step-by-step instructions on how to resolve the problem of lead paint in the home. It is downloadable in a PDF format at **www.epa.gov/lead/pubs/leadsafetybk.pdf**.

In a response to the health hazards that lead paint can create, there are new laws coming into effect to address these concerns. On April 22, 2008, the EPA created a ruling that requires the practice of more stringent lead-safe work habits in an effort to lessen the possibility of lead poisoning. Contractors who are renovating or repairing buildings that have lead paint in them will need to be certified and trained to perform the work in a specific manner to make sure the occupants are not contaminated.

These new laws are scheduled to be fully implemented by April 22, 2010. This new law has direct impact on how builders and renovators work to remove lead paint. Be aware of these new EPA requirements and guidelines. To learn more about this initiative, visit the EPA's "Lead: Renovation, Repair, and Painting" program Web site at **www.epa.gov/fedrgstr/EPA-TOX/2008/April/Day-22/t8141.htm**.

To locate the regional office of the EPA and to learn about specific lead paint programs and initiatives in each state, go online and find the state office at their Web site, **www.epa.gov/lead/pubs/leadoff1.htm**. In addition, the EPA has more detailed information for homeowners on how to renovate their homes if there is lead paint or the suspicion of lead paint in the home. The online link to this brochure is **www.epa.gov/lead/pubs/renovaterightbrochure.pdf**.

Other Environmental Issues to Consider

The following is a list of some of the other environmental issues that you might need to respond to and resolve during the renovation, restoration, and repair of an older home:

- Runoff from storm water.
- Dredge and wetlands.
- Prevention of oil spills.
- Solid waste, which can include both hazardous and non-hazardous materials.
- Hazardous substances to keep off your property or how to properly handle and dispose of them if they are on your property.
- Polychlorinated biphenyl (PCBs), which are manmade chlorinated hydrocarbons. Although no longer manufactured, they can last a long time in soil, and exposure can create serious health risks such as cancer. The EPA presents information about proper handling, storage, and disposal of PCBs at **www.epa.gov/epa-waste/hazard/tsd/pcbs/index.htm**.
- Air quality of the home.
- Animals that are included in the Endangered Species Act. Take care not to harm or disturb them. To learn more, visit the U.S. Fish and Wildlife Service Web site at **www.fws.gov/endangered**.

CHAPTER 3

The Tools and Skills of the Trade

Tools and Skills Needed

There are different schools of thought on whether a homeowner needs home repair experience when taking on a renovation project. Generally speaking, it is beneficial to have some building skills and familiarity with tools when taking on a substantial home renovation project yourself. To get this experience, try doing small repair projects to build confidence and skill level — for example, painting a room, fixing a leaky faucet, replacing the hoses to a washing machine, or wrapping the pipes with insulation. Reading or watching home improvement television book and programs provides a good background.

Take advantage of the instructional classes offered by the large home-building retail stores. Knowledgeable staff will explain how to design a kitchen, tile a bathroom floor, repair a leaky faucet, or plant an herb garden. Merchandisers know that offering a free class gets customers into the store to see their merchandise.

A good rule of thumb — If you cannot do a job almost as well as a professional, then is better to let the professional do the job.

There are some projects that are best left to the professionals. If you think you are in over your head, then you are. For legal reasons, some homeowners will not be able to do certain projects on their homes because state building codes dictate that certain types of construction and renovations must be done by a licensed or certified professional. Unless you are licensed or certified in a project area (e.g., an electrician or plumber), you will need to hire a professional. If you botch the job, then it will have to be re-done, which adds to the cost — plus, it will take longer to complete the work.

Skills and Attributes Needed for a Home Renovation

- **Be realistic about the project when it comes to your skill set and timeframe** — Know what you are capable of, and know when you need to ask for help.

- **Have confidence in yourself and a desire to see the project through to the end.**

- **Possess good project management skills** — Be prepared to solve problems and conflicts as they arise.

- **Have good negotiation skills** — This is important not only at the time of contract negotiations, or when bidding out a job or managing contractors or subcontractors, but throughout the duration of the project. There are times you will need to renegotiate and make decisions when complications arise. Remain in control of the project, even though others are doing the work.

- **Have the ability to forge positive relationships with professionals on your team as well as suppliers of materials** — Open and honest communication helps. Keep on top of what others are doing. Check the work site daily, if possible. If the work is not done to your satisfaction, communicate your concerns early so they can be rectified quickly.

- **Make sure you are physically fit for the challenge** — This kind of work is demanding. You should have the strength to lift work materials; stand for long stretches; bend, kneel, and crawl for extended periods of time; climb ladders and stairs; and face weather extremes.

- **Have the ability to do basic math** — Math skills are beneficial when it comes to measuring and ordering the right amount of supplies and materials.

- **Be organized and neat** — This goes for the paperwork, bids, contracts, invoices, and the work site. Purchase a small file cabinet or briefcase to store project materials. Keep the materials at the work site or someplace safe.

- **Prepare your family to see less of you during the project, but be sure to get their support.**

- **Have patience, especially when there are problems.**

- **Have the ability to say "no."**

- **Have a sense of humor when things go wrong — because they will.**

- **Have the heart of a do-it-yourselfer** — If you are doing the work, are you handy and resourceful, or clumsy and afraid of power tools?

If the latter is true, then consider working side-by-side with a more skilled craftsperson as an apprentice (if she is willing to accommodate the request). If you have the skills and attributes listed above, then you are a great candidate for a home renovation project.

Tools for Your Project

The following is a comprehensive list of tools arranged by project function. It is not necessary to buy all these tools on the first day of the project; investing in the basics is sufficient. Tell those who will be giving you a gift for your birthday, Christmas, or any other gift-giving occasion to buy a tool, and tell them exactly what you want.

It is also not necessary to buy all-new tools. A great way to accumulate a good collection of tools is by inheriting cast-offs or duplicates from family, friends, and neighbors. They will also have some sentimental value. Another great resource for finding tools is at yard sales, flea markets, and auctions. You can find some great tools at thrift shops and secondhand stores, too.

If you like antiques, it is nice to add a few antique or vintage tools to your collection. Some may or may not work, but they are fun to have around. Warning: Collecting antique tools can become habit-forming, and you may end up spending all the money you save on the project buying antique tools.

Tool List from A to Z

The first tool needed is a camera. It does not have to be a fancy one, but make sure before-and-after pictures are taken of renovation projects. They will be great memories for years to come as you brag about all the work you did when renovating your home. Plus, you will see the progression in your skill set as time goes by.

Tools can be purchased at the local hardware store, home-building supply store, catalogs, over the Internet, and through smaller specialty stores like a woodworking shop. Do not hesitate to ask the sales clerk for more information on tools you are thinking about buying or for a demonstration, when possible. Many of the larger home building stores offer classes, and here is a good place to see how some tools are being used.

Carpentry tools

Carpenter's scriber — A tool used to mark where wood needs to be cut.

Chalk line — This is used to create a straight line connecting two points.

Clamps — 6-inch spring clamps and C-clamps; buy at least four of each.

Framing squares — This is an L-shaped tool used for determining right angles when cutting rafters:

- **Steel square** — This tool is used to keep things perpendicular. It is also handy for measuring.

- **Combination square** — A device with a 6-inch steel tool used to mark 45- and 90-degree angles.

Hammers —

- **Claw hammer** — The most common type of hammer used in construction. The head should be made of steel. The face is used to drive nails, and the other end has a two-pronged claw used to remove nails. The handle can be made of fiberglass, wood, or steel. A good, all-purpose claw hammer weighs about 16 ounces and has a 16-inch handle. The claw hammer is best for finer carpentry work versus demolition work.

- **Mallet** — This hammer-like tool is made of either a rubber or wood head. It is used for soft impact drives and will not damage the surface. It is often used with chisels.

- **Small tack hammer** — A lightweight hammer used for driving small nails or brads.

Hatchet — A handheld axe with a short handle.

Levels — These are used to help make sure a wall, floor, or any flat surface is level. They come in different sizes: 30-inch, three-bubble square level (has three glass bubbles filled with liquid so various surfaces can be made level), and a small, multi-function laser level to make a straight line between two points.

Measuring devices:

- **Folding 6-foot wooden ruler.**
- **Steel tape measure** — 12-foot to 16-foot.

Nail set —Used to place nail heads below the wood's surface, it is a short, blunt metal shaft. Place the blunt end on the nail set on the nail head and strike the other end with a hammer.

Pencil compass — A tool used to scribe (draw) circles, contours, and marks.

Pencils — No. 2 work best.

Planes — These are used to smooth the surface of woodwork by paring shavings from it.

- **Block plane** — A small, low-angle plane (with the blade at a low pitch) used to finish off rough edges and to cut across the grain of wood.

- **Jack plane** — A tool used to smooth rough boards and flatten uneven surfaces.

Pliers — Tin snips, linesman's, vise-grip, Channel Lock®, or slip-joint and side cutters.

Plumb bob — This tool is used to find a point directly beneath another point; for instance, it can be used when building a flight of stairs.

Putty knives — 6-inch broad knife and 1½-inch putty knife.

Rasps — These are files made specifically for shaping wood. Four-in-one rasps provides four tools in one with two rounded sides and two flat files.

Sandpaper — There are different grits of sandpaper for different types of sanding jobs. Some sanding begins with coarse paper and ends with fine paper. Purchase a variety of grits and have them on hand for different jobs. Sandpaper grits are designated by a numerical designation: coarse (50 and 60 grit); medium (80 and 100 grit); fine (120 grit), and extra fine (220 grit.)

Saws — There are several sizes, styles, and types of saws available. Each has its own specific purpose. The following are the key ones a renovator should consider purchasing:

- **Backsaw** — Used for fine or accurate cuts.

- **Coping saw** — A fine-bladed saw used for coping moldings.

- **Dovetail saw** — A small saw used for the fine and clean cuts needed for cutting dovetails.

- **Hand saw (panel saw)** — Known for its portability, ease of use, and efficiency, this is the most common handsaw. Its blade is about 2 feet long and tapers from the handle heel to its toe. There are two types: 1. *rip saw,* which cuts in the direction of the grain, and 2. *crosscut,* which cuts across the grain and has twice as many teeth as the rip saw. Both are ideal for cutting large, wide, or thick pieces of wood. Use an 8-inch for rough work and 10-inch for finish work.

- **Japanese saw** — This saw has teeth on both sides of its thin blade and has a rattan handle. The design lets the user cut with a pull stroke, which results in less work and a more accurate cut.

- **Keyhole saw** — A saw that typically has a 6-inch narrow blade, used to cut drywall, plastic, cement board, and soft woods.

- **Miter box** — This tool is an open box with slats that allow a saw to cut moldings and other fine cuts at 45- and 90-degree angles. It is an old-fashioned tool, but it still has many uses. The power miter saws are too powerful for the fine work, especially moldings.

Sawhorses — They are good for creating flat surfaces. Put some heavy-duty plywood or an old door on top of two or three sawhorses, and you have an instant table or work surface. These can also serve as storage shelves for supplies and tools. Homemade or store-bought sawhorses work fine, but make sure they are sturdy enough to hold considerable weight.

Screwdrivers —

- **Regular flathead** — One for large screws and one for small screws (2).

- **Phillips head** — One for large screws and one for small screws.
- **One interchangeable multi-head screwdriver.**

Staple gun — Heavy-duty (buy extra staples).

Stepladder — A stepladder is a short folding ladder with a small platform. A 6-foot high ladder is a good height to reach high places and is best to have as a small, handy platform to place paint, tools, or supplies.

Utility knife — This is a must for anyone doing work around the house. It is a hand-held razor blade in a holder. The blade is adjustable to expose more or less of the blade point. Make sure to buy an extra package of blades to keep on hand so that when the blade is dull, it can quickly be replaced.

Wood chisels — This is a hand-held tool that has a sharp, wedge-shaped end used for shaping, chipping, and removing wood, masonry products, and other building materials. It has a head that is driven with a hammer. It is best to buy the following sizes: ¼-inch, ½-inch, ¾-inch, and 1 inch.

Demolition, pulling, wrecking, and ripping tools

Brooms — Get a heavy-duty push broom and a standard corn- or nylon-bristle house broom to clean up light and heavy debris.

Cat's paw — A small crowbar used to work in tight places or for small tasks.

Cold chisel — This is a versatile tool that has a steel blade with a tempered edge and a handle. It is used to cut and shape wrought iron, aluminum, and sheet metal, or to remove rivets, bolts, and nails. Other uses include removing the mortar from the joints of a brick wall, or removing ceramic tiles from a floor or wall. There are various sizes and designs (used in masonry projects), and some varieties come with a rubber safety handle.

Crowbar — A tool made from forged steel, used to pry things apart and remove nails. It is about 2 feet in length; one end is shaped like a hook, and the other has a flat, chisel-like shape.

Drop cloths — These are used to cover objects or the floor (to keep it clean and clear of debris). Available in cloth or plastic.

Dustpan and brush — Get a large metal dustpan and heavy-duty brush.

Gooseneck wrecking bar — A heavy-duty crow bar used for demolition and pulling out nails. It makes demolition jobs easier. The flat end has a nail-puller, and the curved end is used to pry objects. Get one short bar of 14 inches, and one large bar of 24 inches.

Hacksaw — A small, hand-held saw with fine teeth, used to cut metal.

Headlamp — Battery-powered. Good for dark spots where you need two free hands.

Kneepads — Padded accessory used to protect knees when kneeling on the floor for an extended period of time.

Mallet — A hammer with a head made out of wood to hit objects, but the softness of the wood will not scar the object being struck.

Masking tape — A general all-purpose tape used for bundling, sealing, and masking. Adheres to many surfaces; it is easy to cut and easy to remove.

Pry bars — Used for pulling and wrecking materials by using leverage.

Shovel — The scoop-style shovel is ideal for picking up piles of debris, sand, gravel, and snow. Usually made out of aluminum with a wooden handle.

Sledgehammer — A large and heavy hammer with a head made out of forged steel and a long wooden or fiberglass handle. It is used to break through walls and comes in handy on many demolition projects. Wear safety glasses when using this tool.

Trash barrels — Galvanized metal or heavy-duty plastic.

Drill bits: High-quality bits for wood, metal, and masonry

Center punch — This steel rod has a pointed end and is useful when making an indentation in a wooden or metal surface. This tool makes it easier to help start the hole before using an electric drill.

Hole saw — A spade drill bit used to enlarge existing holes or to drill new round holes, usually about 1¼ inch in diameter.

Large-twist drill bits — These bits are used for drilling metal.

Masonry bits — These drill bills are used to drill holes in concrete, brick, marble, stone and granite. They have harder shanks and tips to handle the harder surfaces they drill into.

Plumber's bit kit — This kit includes different size bits to accommodate drilling the larger holes involved in plumbing projects. The sizes match the various sizes of pipes used in plumbing. It is more affordable to buy bits in a kit than to buy them individually.

Reamers — A bit used to enlarge a hole or make a more accurate shape.

Vix® bits — These drill bits are very precise and are used specifically to bore pilot screw holes in metal hinges and latches. These drill bits help the user properly center drilling holes for hinges and latches used on doors and cabinetry. This makes the installation of hardware easier, more accurate, and more uniform.

Electrical tools

Cable ties — Plastic cable ties can come in handy when it is necessary to tie several wires together. Get a bag of these accessories to use on electrical and other projects. They typically come in sizes between 4-inch to 60-inch, and in both lightweight and heavy-duty strengths. If possible, buy a variety of sizes and strengths.

Cordless drill — This tool works the same as an electric drill but gets its power from a rechargeable battery.

Crimping pliers — These are used to crimp electrical connectors or electrical terminals. They come in a ratchet style, which is versatile and makes tasks easier. There are crimping pliers that offer interchangeable heads so they can crimp different-sized connectors and terminals.

Diagonal cutters — These pliers can cut, and the diagonal cutting edges provides leverage to pull cotter pins.

Electrical tape — This adhesive tape is used to insulate electrical wires. It comes in a variety of colors, but black is the standard used for most electrical work. The different-color tapes can be used to indicate the phase and purpose of the wire, as well as the voltage. The tape is made in both plastic and vinyl, but the vinyl is more flexible. The tape is wrapped tightly around wires to insulate them from exposure to the elements and prevent anyone from touching live wires. Ultraviolet black tape is used to cover wires that will be exposed to sunlight.

Electrical voltage testers — This is a meter that tests whether there is electrical power at electrical outlets or wires. This is an electrician's best friend.

First, use the tester on an outlet or wire where there is electrical service to make sure the tester works. Second, shut the power off where the work needs to be done. Third, test the outlet or wires you plan to work on to make sure there is no electricity. Each tester will have different indicators for whether there is electricity in an outlet. They come in different styles and prices. It is not necessary to buy an expensive one; one in the price range of about $30 is sufficient.

Fish tape — The tape is a thin and flat piece of wire coiled inside a case that is run through the pipe; the wire is hooked onto the tape and pulled through the pipe to the other end. This tool is used to run cable behind finish surfaces and pull wire into an electrical conduit or pipe.

Flashlight — When the power is off, it is important to have a flashlight to see the work. A headlamp attached to a hat is even better, so both hands can be free.

Hacksaw — A small and inexpensive hand-held saw with very fine teeth, used to cut metal. Comes in handy with electrical and metal work.

Lineman's pliers — These are heavy-duty pliers that cut on the side with leverage.

Needle-nose pliers (long-nose pliers) — The long, pointed nose of these pliers helps to reach into difficult locations to grab, grip, and bend wires. The nose length range in size from 4-inch to 8-inch and can be used to cut wire.

Nippers (end cutters) — This is a hand tool used to cut nails, wire, and other metal. They come in handy when a close and straight cut of a piece of wire is needed.

Slip joint pliers — These pliers range from 4-inch to 10-inch; be sure to get a small and large pair.

Wire nuts or twist-on connectors — These are caps used when splicing together the copper ground wires to create a continuous ground through the electrical system. It is a covering for "hot" wires to prevent electrocution. About ¾-inch of insulation is removed from the wires, and the exposed copper wire is twisted together with the lineman's pliers and screwed into the nut.

Wire strippers — This tool cleanly cuts and pulls off the insulation from electrical wire.

Masonry tools

Cold chisel — This is a versatile tool that has a steel blade and a handle. It can be used to cut and shape metal such as wrought iron, aluminum, and sheet metal. It can help to remove rivets, bolts, and nails. Other uses include removing the mortar from the joints of a brick wall or removing ceramic tiles from a floor or wall. There are various sizes and designs.

Concrete finishing trowel — This finishing tool smoothes and seals wet concrete. It is a flat piece of metal with a wooden handle and comes in different sizes to accommodate different-size projects.

Framing hammer (heavy-duty) — The hammer comes with steel heads that weigh 20 to 32 ounces, or titanium heads that weigh 12 to 16 ounces. They have a wooden handle with a straight claw. They are heavy-duty and are used for framing a house.

Mason's hawk — A rectangular flat surface with a handle under the surface that is perpendicular; it is something you will hold with one hand.

Mason's string — This tool is made out of a heavy string that does not stretch. It is used as a guide in carpentry, masonry, and other construction projects. To use, stretch the mason's string between two ends to establish a flush, level line between ends.

Mason's trowel — A flat trowel that is triangular in shape and used when applying mortar to brick or stone.

Square notched trowel — A rectangular-shaped mason's trowel with notches on two edges. It is used to apply adhesive to a surface, such as the adhesive used to install ceramic tile.

Tile nippers — A tool used to cut and shape ceramic tiles to fit around various shapes.

Miscellaneous tools

Allen wrenches — These are metal, L-shaped, six-sided tools that can drive screws and other fasteners that have recessed hexagonal heads. They come in a set with various sizes.

Caulk gun (and various caulks based on intended use) — Caulk is used as an adhesive bond, to fill and to seal. The caulk gun holds the different tubes of caulk for ease of use.

Flashlight — A high-quality flashlight will come in handy, especially when the electrical power is off. Helps to illuminate basements, behind walls, and attics.

Nylon line — Braided nylon line (rope) is used to tie bundles of wood together, or to tie down materials on a trailer.

Stud finder — There are a few different styles of this tool, which are used to find the studs in a wall when it is covered with a wall covering like drywall (often the brand Sheetrock). One style uses a magnet to detect nails and screws; another uses electromagnetic waves (radar) and reads changes in a wall's density to sense the end of the stud. If the wall has more than one layer of drywall, then the magnetic tool will not work, so it is good to have an electronic radar version. The cost of the magnetic version is nominal ($3 to $20); it is worth purchasing both.

Swanson® Speed® square — Can be used the same as a framing square; it is especially useful to determine the correct angle to cut rafters.

Toolbox — Some are metal, and others are made of heavy-duty plastic. They are available in a variety of sizes, and the choice depends on the number of tools in the box.

Outdoor tools

Digging bar — Ideal for prying or levering heavy objects; also for excavating, breaking, and loosening hard soil, rock, and even concrete.

Garden shovel — Shovels for the garden come in different sizes and lengths. It is good to have one with a long handle and a pointed, sharp edge spade. It is important to keep the edge sharp, or it will not work as well. A lip on top of the shovel blade helps to do the work. The tool should be heavyweight to make the work easier. There are also shovels with rounded spades, as well as small, hand-held garden shovels for small tasks.

Pick — A heavy-duty metal, pointed tool used to dig rocks and roots out of the dirt. It is attached to an axe-style handle so the user can swing it over his head for leverage and power.

Wheelbarrow — A handy, one-wheeled cart used to haul materials.

Painting tools

Combs — Plastic or rubber combs used in the application of decorative finishes to painted surfaces.

Disposable paper masks — These are good to wear when sanding surfaces prior to painting.

Extension handle for roller — These come in sectional wooden pieces so that the user can adjust the length; helps to extend the length of the paint roller for walls and ceilings.

Paint can lid-lifter — A small, metal leveraging tool used to pry off the cover of paint cans.

Paintbrushes — It is best to have different-sized brushes such as 1-inch, 2-inch, and 3-inch brushes for oil-based and latex water-based paints.

Paint roller and roller covers — A paint roller is a metal tool with a wooden or plastic handle, used to paint large, flat areas like paint walls, floors, and ceiling. A cylindrical cover made of napped fabric is placed over the roller. The nap of covers comes in different thicknesses; for example, a stucco wall needs a thicker nap, and a ceiling needs a thinner nap.

Painter's masking tape — A tape used when painting to create a straight edge; although it has an adhesive backing, it does not damage the surfaces it adheres to. It can remain for several days and can pull off surfaces easily.

Paint scraper — A hand-held scraper used in the preparation work prior to painting. It helps remove old paint from wood trim or other surfaces.

Rags — These can be purchased or made from old T-shirts, linens, or other absorbent materials.

Roller pan — A metal or plastic container used to hold paint.

Tarps (or large plastic sheets) — Used to cover floors.

Plumbing tools

Basin wrench — A wrench used to install or remove the mounting or coupling nuts on kitchen or bathroom faucets.

Flange maker — A tool used to flare out the end of a pipe; the flange helps to prevent a coupling and will not come off.

Flux — A paste put on pipes to clean them prior to soldering them.

Pipe cutters — They cut plastic PVC or metal pipes and are available in a variety of sizes.

Plumber's putty — A sealant used to help prevent leaks around drains, toilets, and sinks.

Plumbers sanding paper — Fine-grit sandpaper used to clean corrosion; can also be used to knock burrs off pipes prior to soldering.

Plumber's snake or auger — This is used to clear blocked drains and toilets. It is a long, coiled wire encased in a housing unit with a crank attached to one end and is available in different lengths to fix various clogs.

Plungers — Used to clear sinks and toilets.

Propane — A torch used to thaw out a frozen pipe or melt solder.

Silicone tape — Used to wrap around threaded fittings to seal them and help prevent leaks.

Solder — A soft metal sold as a wire, used to join pipes and fittings.

Stillson wrench — These large, heavy-duty, adjustable wrenches are used for plumbing and demolition projects.

Tongue and groove pliers — Tool comes in different sizes, with wide and adjustable jaws used to grasp, bend, cut, and shape objects. Also called by the manufacturer's name of Channellock® pliers.

Tubing cutter — A handheld tool with a sharp cutting wheel, used to cut soft metals such as copper, aluminum, and brass.

Wire brush — Used to clean metal pipes before soldering or joining together.

Power tools

Circular saw — A power saw with a circular blade sticking out through a flat base. It is ideal for making straight and fast cuts on woods of different thickness. This is possible because the saw blade can be raised and lowered to accommodate the wood being cut.

Compound miter saw — This is also known as a chop saw. It can be used to make straight cuts, but is similar to a miter box in that it can make 45-degree and 90-degree cuts by rotating the tool's turntable. There is a tilt-and-pivot feature on this saw that makes it ideal for cutting crown moldings, picture frames, and other woods that need a beveled edge. Blades range in size from 8 inches to 12 inches.

Cordless drill — This is used the same as a corded drill, but without the electrical cord, and it makes it easier to work on ladders and a damp ground. It does not have the same amount of heavy-duty power of a corded drill but comes in handy if the power is not available.

Electric corded drill (⅜-inch size) — Its basic function is to drill holes and drive screws, but with additional attachments it can sand, grind, and stir.

Extension cords — Get extension cords that are safe and have a UL listed on their tag. Also, get #16 gauge wire cords in both a light-duty and heavy-duty style. Buy these in 50- and 100-foot lengths.

Pneumatic stapler — This is a power tool that saves time by quickly driving staples into materials instead of using a handheld stapler. It requires an air compressor and is ideal on projects such as carpet installation, attaching roof felt, installing floor underlay, and installing various types of insulation. They are also handy when putting together doorjambs and stapling tongue-and-groove boards together.

Radial arm saw — A circular saw rail-mounted to a pivoted arm.

Reciprocating saw — With the ability to cut through metal, wood, or plastics with ease, this saw is well suited for demolition jobs such as wall removal. It also creates a rough opening for use with plumbing and heating ducts projects.

Router — This tool uses bits to form cabinet joints (dado and rabbet), trim plastic laminate, and shape decorative edges and moldings.

Saber saw — This is a portable reciprocating jigsaw that can be used to follow and cut curved or straight lines; different blades allow cuts to metal, plastic, brick, or enclosed holes.

Sanders — There are a variety of different power sanders available, used for different purposes. The following are some good sanders to consider purchasing when renovating an older home. Make sure to have different grits of sandpaper on hand for different types of sanding projects:

- **Belt sander** — With its revolving belt, this sander smoothes and shapes wooden surfaces. It can also be used to strip away paint and finishes.

- **Dremel®** — A small, high-speed rotary power tool that uses bits for grinding, sanding, drilling, polishing, and sharpening.

- **Finishing/block sanders** — This takes longer than the orbit sander but provides a better finish. This gets closer into the corners than a circular orbit sander.

- **Palm sander** — A small, vibrating, handheld sander that can be held with one hand. Can be used for fine and rough sanding; it is best to sand in the direction of the grain.

- **Random orbit sanders** — This is a sander that moves in a circular motion and never sands the same area twice because the disk moves in an elliptical pattern. Ideal for both polishing and sanding; it is not important to go with the grain of the wood.

Table saw — A saw on a table, used to rip long planks of wood.

Wet saw — Good for cutting bricks, pavers, or tiles. A steady stream of water keeps the blade and material being cut cool. It is a little messy to clean up, but well worth the effort.

Rental equipment

Some items might make more sense to rent instead of buy, but this will depend on the length of time the equipment is needed. If only needed for a week or less, it is best to rent. Here are pieces of equipment to consider renting:

Air compressors — This equipment supplies air to pneumatic tools such as nail guns, paint sprayers, staplers, drills, and sanders. It makes big jobs easier by powering tools with air instead of doing all the work by hand. A tank holds pressurized air until it is needed; compressors run on electricity, gas, steam, or manual power.

Dumpsters® — These large metal containers come in different sizes and are used to store waste; they are especially useful during the demolition phase of a project. They are delivered to the work site and removed once the work is complete. Waste management companies rent them and charge their own fees for the service. Compare prices before ordering one.

Floor sanding equipment — This equipment is used to sand hardwood floors. There are different types of sanders: the drum sander, the orbital sander, the disc sander, and the abraders can remove the finished surface without damaging the wood beneath. Several steps are involved in refinishing floors; plus, it takes finesse in learning to use the equipment. Plan to keep the sander for several days, depending on the size of the area to be sanded.

Generators — This piece of equipment provides electricity to remote locations. They come in household, recreation, and commercial work models. Get a commercial-grade generator when renting or buying. This will provide more power for tools and equipment.

Each tool has a wattage requirement needed when starting and running it. For example, a saw may need more wattage when it starts to cut versus when it is turned on. Tool tags should give this information. This is a called a "reactive load," so know this information prior to buying or renting equipment.

Jackhammers — Used to break up concrete walkways and driveways.

Lift jack — This equipment is used to lift materials and tools to a roof, a second story, or any job site that is off the ground. For instance, it can be used to bring heavy shingles onto the roof or, if rebuilding a brick chimney, it can be used to transport the old and new bricks easily.

Spray painting equipment — Equipment used to paint interior and exterior surfaces. Spray guns work with pressurized air to distribute a thin and even coat of paint to the surface. There are different sizes and styles available, depending on the nature of the project.

Staging/scaffolding — Ladders and planks used as construction/work platforms. They can be set up inside and outside. Used for painting, roof repair, installation of gutters, and for any projects high enough off the ground where a standard ladder cannot be used. Rental companies can set up and remove the scaffolding when the work is complete.

Tractors — A tractor is a heavy-duty piece of equipment used for many outdoor projects. Different attachments can be used with the tractor when a project requires digging, scooping, pushing, and cutting. For example, a front loader is attached to the front of tractor to move gravel, dirt, sand, debris, or other material around the property.

> Work shoes should be heavy-duty, with thick soles to prevent nail penetration. Also, getting a tetanus shot before starting projects is recommended.

Safety tools

First-aid kit — These kits can be purchased with basic items that can be used in case of a minor accident or injury. For example, the American Red Cross offers a variety of kits from their Web site store at **www.redcross-store.org/dp.aspx?pgid=-1**. For those who prefer to assemble their own kits, the American Red Cross suggests these basic items:

- Tweezers, scissors, and oral thermometer

- A blanket and instant cold compress

- Individually wrapped assorted sizes and shapes of bandages, rolls of bandage, and sterile gauze pads

- Adhesive cloth tape

- Absorbent compress dressings

- Non-latex gloves, antiseptic wipes, and ointment; hydrocortisone ointment and aspirin

- Plastic breathing barrier with a one-way valve to perform CPR

Hard hat — A construction-type hat made of hard plastic, used during demolition or other renovation projects where debris could fly. Remember, it will not protect unless you wear it.

Hearing protectors — The American National Standards Institute (ANSI) and the Acoustic Society of America have determined and approved, through guideline ANSI S3.19-1974, a specific style of disposable foam earplugs that mold to the shape of the ear canal or earmuffs.

Buy a whole box and place in ears when using loud power tools or doing other tasks that are loud. Look for the ANSI code on the box.

Nail apron — A leather or canvas apron where nails, screws, and other small items can be stored while working.

Nose/mouth filter mask — A protective mask that keeps out dust, sand, paint chips, and pollutants.

Respirator masks — These prevent unwanted and unhealthy fumes and particles from entering the body through the nasal passages and mouth. Good to use if working in the area of asbestos products.

Safety goggles or glasses — These should meet the guidelines of the ANSI, which approved Z87.1-2003 as a replacement for Z87.1-1989 (R-1998) specifications; devices that meet the "high" impact criteria are marked "Z87+."

Work gloves — A heavy-duty glove made of leather or cloth to protect hands when picking up debris; they also help to grip and grab objects.

Salvage Pantry

A salvage pantry is where vintage, antique, or period architectural materials can be stored until work begins on your renovation project. In your travels to antique shops, salvage yards, architectural warehouses, Dumpsters, demolition sites, thrift shops, yard sales, and estate sales, look for items that are appropriate for restoring an older home. Ideally, it is best to have a storage shed or large corner in the garage or basement where the treasures can be stored.

Antique or older materials might have been painted with lead paint, and plumbing fixtures might have lead pipes. Know the health hazards of lead and other contaminants when purchasing older elements. Keep your health and that of your family safe — do not bring these items into your home.

Also, most wooden items that are older will not be pressure-treated. If they are to be used outside, beware — they will not stand up to the elements as long as today's pressure-treated lumbers can.

Look for the following items to put in the pantry:

- Wooden doors (interior, exterior, and screen) that fit in with the period of the house being renovated
- Windows
- Hardware, doorknobs, and hinges

- Moldings, trim, rosette blocks, and ornamental moldings
- Mantels, fireplace grates, and equipment
- Light fixtures and chandeliers (will need to be rewired with more current wires)
- Posts, shutters, and balusters
- Bathroom sinks, fixtures, and faucets
- Cabinetry and cabinet doors
- Switch plates and door plates
- Decorative brackets
- Bricks, marble, and concrete ornamental pieces
- Register grates and coal grates
- Iron gates and decorative iron and wooden fences
- Period accent pieces
- Embossed tin ceiling tiles or sheets
- Any other items that might fit into an older home

If you are a packrat by nature, then buying and storing salvage materials could turn out to be a storage problem. Keep buying habits to a minimum to keep surplus materials from taking over any free space and becoming an eyesore. It is helpful to be neat and organized. If not, discipline yourself to keep materials in categories to easily spot them.

CASE STUDY: HABITAT FOR HUMANITY'S RESTORE

Kim Schick
Manager for seven years
606 East Main Street
Lebanon, TN 37087
615-453-3799

A great place to find building materials, appliances, architectural elements, and period fixtures are from the Habitat for Humanity ReStore. These are retail stores that are affiliated with the non-profit organization Habitat for Humanity. They can be found in many metropolitan, urban, and rural areas, and they offer quality new and used supplies and materials for homeowners to purchase at reduced prices.

Sales proceeds go into the building fund, which is used to build Habitat for Humanity houses. One detail Kim Schick wishes to point out is "the ReStore is open to the general public and is not just a resource for those involved in building (or buying) a Habitat for Humanity house." Everything is donated and is an alternative venue for residential and commercial property owners and do-it-yourselfers to shop. Local and national retailers, contractors, and the general public donate the entire inventory available for purchase.

After being the manager of a ReStore, Schick has had many interesting items donated to her location. "The most unique item was an East Lake door. This was an intricately carved wooden door made in the turn of the century that was a real beauty," Schick said.

With 169 new appliances sitting in their warehouse, a national appliance manufacturer made the decision to donate them to Schick's store. Because of the weakened situation of the economy, the manufacturer knew it would be beneficial to donate the product rather than have it stored away in the warehouse. "We could offer these greatly sought-after units at an attractive price, and the manufacturer gets a tax write-off. So it is a win-win situation for everyone involved," Schick said.

One of the newest ways that the Restore obtains inventory is to deconstruct a house. If someone has an old house they plan to tear down, they should consider getting in touch with their local Habitat for Humanity office to see if they would be interested in deconstructing the house. This means Habitat for Humanity would send a team of volunteers to remove all the salvageable building materials and fixtures to later sell in their ReStore. As Schick points out, "This is a green thing. It is a great way to reduce the amount of refuse going into landfills and offers vintage and period materials to the general public for re-use in their properties." Additionally, property owners receive a tax write-off for donating items.

The typical customers visiting Schick's ReStore are do-it-yourself homeowners and landlords. "There are many regulars stopping by on a daily or weekly basis to check out the new inventory. I also see shoppers who are trying to flip a house they recently purchased," Schick said. In order to get back into the housing market after buying a house at a low price, some will attempt to renovate and repair their home to the best of their ability by using affordable, high-quality materials. This way, they can sell at a high price and make a profit.

One of the most typical items donated are doors. "Many homeowners upgrade their doors as a home improvement project, so I get lots of doors in. Then landlords replace doors often on rental units, so I often see them coming in to find doors to replace damaged or outdated doors," Schick said.

Schick said that was how a recently married couple arrived at the store one day. They were looking for windows to replace the old, rickety ones in their newly purchased home. They were hauling a horse trailer around North Carolina and Tennessee and visiting all of the ReStores in search of period materials and fixtures to use on their older home. The interesting part of the story is how they were spending their honeymoon.

"They were able to find exactly the right style and sizes of windows they needed," Schick said. "They carefully packed them in the horse trailer and left to go to the next ReStore on their list. But before leaving, they told me that our ReStore had the best prices, and they were glad they stopped here on their trek."

To find the ReStores in the United States, visit the Habitat for Humanity Web site at **www.habitat.org/cd/env/restores.aspx**. Once a renovation project is finished, donate excess building materials, either new or used, to the local Habitat ReStore. Make sure you get a receipt and use the donation as a charitable contribution on your taxes.

CHAPTER 4

Get a Helping Hand, then Get a Start

Assistance While Renovating Historic Homes

If your home is located in a historic district, or if it is designated as a historic place, there might be financial incentives to restore and preserve the home. Assistance could come in the form of tax benefits, grants, or professional guidance from historic preservationists affiliated with federal, state, and local agencies, as well as historic societies or commissions.

Federal, State, and Local Programs for Historic Homes

The National Historic Preservation Act was adopted in 1966, and its main purpose is to identify, evaluate, and protect historic properties. This program is part of the mandate of the Secretary of the Interior's department and falls under the auspices of the National Historic Preservation Act's Section 110. This requires all federal agencies to establish their own historic preservation programs.

The National Register of Historic Places Web site is located at **www.nps. gov/nr**. This is a list of the nation's historic places that have been worthy of preservation. There are more than 80,000 properties listed, which represent more than 1.4 million individual buildings, sites, districts, structures, and objects.

Determining eligibility

It is well worth determining whether a property currently owned or being considered for purchase would fall within the parameters of a federal historic restoration program in your state. Each state oversees the federal guidelines of the National Parks Service's programs and will have specific programs and initiatives. If you think your property has historic significance, even if it is not in a historic district, then submit a nomination to the State's Historic Preservation Office (SHPO). If the property is approved, it will be listed on the National Register. A few key considerations:

- To determine eligibility, the property needs to be examined for its age, integrity, and historic significance.

- You will need to complete a nomination form; the SHPO will review it and determine eligibility through a rigorous process. The state can offer assistance with completing the application, but the National Park Service makes the final listing decision.

- A property owner is not obligated to participate, even if his or her home is deemed historic. Yet there are benefits, such as an increase in property value, which might impact the resale value of the home and other incentives.

- If you are planning to renovate, repair, or remodel, check with the SHPO in your area for state or local preservation laws that could impact the project.

Understand the program

Understand the guidelines of the local National Historic Preservation programs in your city or town, especially if your property is a historic place or in a historic district. Contact the local preservation group and ask if they have written guidelines. If they do not have available guidelines, make an effort to meet with a representative and learn as much as you can prior to making any exterior renovations. Know the specifications of what is expected of a property owner, and know the protocol for meeting with the historic society to present your proposal.

If the plan is to make an older home look like a newer home, or to add an addition that is contemporary in style, it is best not to buy property in a historic area. There is a good chance that you will always be at odds with the historic board or society. Societies must adhere to the federal program guidelines, or they could lose their status as a historic district or place. They will require homeowners to follow these guidelines and restrictions, as most people who serve on these boards have a love of the history of a place and want to preserve it.

To determine if a house is eligible for the National Historic list, contact your state office by visiting the National Register of Historic Places Web site at **www.nps.gov/history/nr/shpolist.htm**.

When contacting your local SHPO, request information, research materials, and the necessary forms to begin the nomination process for the National Register.

The Federal Historic Preservation Tax Incentives Program

The Federal Historic Tax Incentives Program encourages individuals to purchase and rehabilitate historic properties that will be used as income-producing investment properties. These properties can be used as rental units, business locations, and any other income-producing purpose. This particular tax incentive is not available for the rehabilitation of historic properties that are being used as a private residence.

The one exception is if a portion of the private residence is to be used for a rental unit or a business. The incentive is offered in the form of a tax credit — not a tax deduction. Though both benefit the taxpayer directly, a tax credit decreases the amount of tax she pays, and a tax deduction lessens the amount of income liable to be taxed.

Tax laws change periodically, so keep on top of any tax changes through a tax advisor to make sure a property is eligible for any credit, or visit the IRS Web site at **www.irs.gov** to see what is new. There are two types of tax incentives available:

1. If a property is a certified historic property and it is commercial, industrial, or used as residential rental units, then they will qualify for a 20 percent investment tax credit. A tax credit is a 20 percent rebate based on the costs of the rehabilitation/restoration. The rebate offsets some of the unique costs inherent to renovating an historic property. The National Park Service runs this program and certifies the rehabilitation/restoration. All of the 50 states have their own technical services staff, and they will help the property owners during the application and review phase of the process.

2. The second incentive is a 10 percent investment tax credit rebate for properties that are non-historic and put into service before 1936. This credit is only for properties being used for non-residential purposes..The building must not have been moved from its original location after 1935 to be eligible. Use IRS Tax Form 3468 to claim this credit in the year the building was put into service after it was rehabilitated.

The National Register of Historic Places does not offer the tax incentive program. Instead, the Heritage Preservation Services, which is a division of the National Park Service, manages the day-to-day activities of this tax credit program. In addition, the local SHPO and the IRS assist in the program, too.

Key eligibility terms for the program

- The historic building must appear in the National Register of Historic Places or have certification as providing to the importance of a "registered historic district."

- After rehabilitation, the historic building must be used for a minimum of five years to generate income. Residential properties occupied by owners cannot receive the federal rehabilitation tax credit.

It is required for the project to meet the "substantial rehabilitation test" — the rehabilitation cost must be greater than the cost of pre-rehabilitation. For a project going through multiple stages of completion, the test needs to be met within two to five years. All rehabilitation work should be conducted according to the rehabilitation standards set by the Secretary of the Interior. The following ten principles guarantee a building has maintained its historic character throughout the rehabilitation process:

1. The use of the property will be for its intended historic purpose. Otherwise, it will be put into a new use that needs little alteration to the characteristics that define the building, as well as the site and surrounding environment.

2. The property's historic nature will be maintained and preserved. There will be no discarding of historic materials or changes in the features and spaces defining the property.

3. Each property will serve as its own physical record of time, place, and use. The property will not undergo alterations that falsify its historical development, including attaching architectural elements or features from different buildings.

4. Although most properties undergo changes throughout time, these changes will be well kept and maintained because they have achieved historic significance.

5. Distinctive features, finishes, and construction techniques or examples of craftsmanship that define a historic property will remain intact.

6. Historic characteristics with a decline in quality will be fixed. If this repair is severe in nature, the replacement feature will replicate the original in design, color, texture, other visual elements and, when possible, materials. When conducting replacements, this must be documented, either physically or with pictorial evidence.

7. The use of chemical or physical treatments, including sandblasting, is prohibited. Surfaces will be cleaned when deemed appropriate, and even then using the most sensitive means available.

8. Substantial archaeological resources impacted by a project will be maintained and protected. If disturbances are necessary, measures of mitigation will take place.

9. When new additions, outer changes, or relatively new construction takes place, defining historic components of the property will not be ruined. The new work will differ from the old. In order to shield the historic integrity of the property as well as the surrounding environment, both works will be compatible in terms of the massing, size, scale, and architectural features.

10. When the property undergoes new additions or relatively new construction, this will be conducted in such a manner that if removed in the future, the property will retain its imperative form, and the integrity of the historic property and environment will remain intact.

To learn more about the tax credit program, visit these Web sites:

- The National Park Service: **www.nps.gov/history/hps/tps/tax**
- National Conference of State Historic Preservation Officers: **www.ncshpo.org**
- The Internal Revenue Service: **www.nps.gov/history/hps/tps/tax/IRS.htm**

Historic Societies and Commissions

Many communities have their own historical societies that can assist in a historic restoration. The Web site **www.DAddezio.com** offers help in researching family genealogy; they also have a database of historical societies that can be searched by state. To find a local society, visit the Web site at **www.DAddezio.com/society/hill**.

The American Association for State and Local History has state-by-state listings of historical information about houses, neighborhoods, and communities. To find state resources, agencies, and organizations, visit the Web site at **www.aaslh.org/cgi-bin/statelinks.cgi**.

Assistance for Rural Homeowners

The U.S. Department of Agriculture (USDA) offers assistance and programs to rural Americans to improve, make safer/sanitary, and modernize their homes through renovation and repair. This assistance is funded by the government and comes through the Rural Housing Repair and Rehabilitation Loan Program, also known as the Section 504 Program. This is a program for families who have low incomes and meet the eligibility guidelines. The money can be used for repairs, renovations, or to make the home accessible for the disabled. The Housing & Community Facilities Program (HCFP) offers two assistance opportunities:

1. If a low-income rural homeowner is 62 years or older, she can apply for a home improvement grant (as long as she cannot afford to pay a Section 504 loan).

2. A low-income family can apply for a Section 504 government loan with 1 percent interest for 20 years to repair, improve, and make a home safe.

The payback period is up to 20 years, and there are little or no application or closing costs; however, there are some requirements and guidelines, such as all work must meet local building codes. To learn more about the program, visit the USDA's HCFP Web site at **www.rurdev.usda.gov/rHS/ common/indiv_intro.htm**.

Nuts and Bolts (Where to Begin)

For some, the American dream is still home ownership. According to the 2007 U.S. Census Bureau report, 68 percent of Americans own a home in the United States. West Virginia had the greatest rate of home ownership in 2007, at 77.6 percent. Home ownership is a milestone and the beginning of a new phase in most people's lives, although there are those who go to the next level and are able to buy an additional home for investment purposes or as a weekend or vacation retreat.

The topics covered in this section are relevant for anyone thinking about buying a home, anyone already living in a home, or anyone planning to sell a home. Buying and selling homes for profit is a viable business for anyone who can learn from his or her mistakes. As much information as there is available in books like this one, everyone makes mistakes in either paying too much for the property, underestimating the cost of the repairs, or hiring the wrong professional to do the work. One of the best ways to make a profit in selling a home is to do as much preparation, research, and planning prior to the purchase and renovation.

Setting priorities and goals will also be contingent on the purpose of the house. If the house is your primary residence, your priorities will be different from if you were renovating the house to sell. If you are renovating your house to sell for profit, your design and renovation plans will appeal to the general consumer and have fewer details that reflect your personal taste and styles.

The work on a renovation project will be either "structural" or "cosmetic" — or you can think in terms of "serious" or "fun." The structural projects need to be done first. Begin to set priorities and goals with the following scheme:

1. Divide the projects into two sections: structural and cosmetic.
2. From this preliminary exercise, look at the structural renovations and repairs, and determine which should come first.

It does not make sense to pull in a new bathroom if the floor joists cannot handle the weight of the project because termites have done damage. Ascertain how secure the structural integrity of the property is so you can address these repairs early on. Safety and health concerns need to be at the top of the list to protect the people living in it and those who will work on it. Think of the following:

- If buying a house that will need renovations, and if securing financing for those renovations, be sure to have enough after the down payment to pay for these top-priority projects.

- Money will dictate when certain projects can be done. The l eaky roof needs attention before the recessed lighting in the walk-in closet.

- Become familiar with the local codes and regulations, and adhere to them.

- Set goals for projects that have tentative beginning and ending dates.

Refer to the Evaluation Checklist in the Appendix, which is a list of all the aspects of a home inspection. This checklist helps a homeowner evaluate the condition of their home.

Creating the Budget

Start to prepare the budget by listing all the needed renovations. If the home has just been purchased and there is a home inspection report, then use this as a reference tool to list the projects from most important to least important. Even if this report is a few years old, it can still be used as guide.

When creating a budget for the renovation project, plan to add 10 to 20 percent for unforeseen changes, problems, and mistakes. Even adding as much as 30 percent to the budget will ensure there will be enough money to complete the project. If receiving financing for the work, it is best to get as much money up-front and try to avoid returning to the lender to ask for more money.

Getting estimates and staying organized

Once a list of projects is ranked according to priority, it is time to estimate the costs of the renovations. If a general contractor is managing the project, he or she will generate an estimate of costs. If the homeowner acts as the general contractor, then he can get estimates from subcontractors. For smaller projects that only require materials, get estimates on all the materials needed.

Estimating repairs and renovations can include the following actions:

- **If it is a cosmetic repair, such as painting, and you plan to do the work yourself, go to a home improvement store** — Also try to look at their Web stores and estimate the cost of the materials and supplies. Have a budget for every project big and small.

- **Always get two to three written estimates** — For major systems, such as a central heat and air system, have two to three professionals prepare an estimate. In some cases it might not be possible to get three estimates, but always try to get two for comparative purposes.

- **If the house needs a new roof, get two estimates** — To save money, have the roofer also prepare an estimate on labor only. Then buy materials directly from the roofing supplier and get the materials delivered to the site on your own. Most roofers can provide a supply list once they measure the job.

- **Be as organized and efficient as possible in getting and keeping track of estimates** — Doing your work on a computer or another electronic storage device is fine. Having a laptop is an option because it is easy to bring along. Perhaps a notebook or a binder works well to keep track of documents, brochures, and estimates. The method of recordkeeping and using other techniques to stay organized is a personal preference.

- **Once the project begins, organization is imperative** — Keep track of contracts, receipts, telephone numbers, and schedules. This alleviates wasting time and energy, and helps to get ready for the trade professionals and scheduled deliveries.

How to finance

Paying with cash might result in getting better deals and having more leverage when the market is tight. This can be true for both buying real estate and renovating a home.

When borrowing, it is important to be both cautious and realistic about the amount needed. There is a balancing act between borrowing enough money to finish the work and not borrowing too much to jeopardize a credit score and the ability to pay other debts. There is nothing wrong with doing projects in stages, as long as the living environment in the home is safe and healthy. We can all live with an ugly environment temporarily, but living broke can be miserable.

Financial resources for renovations

- **Use savings** — As a general rule, do not use more than 50 percent of savings unless it is specifically earmarked for renovations.

- **Save until there is enough cash for each specific renovation project** — This approach might mean it takes longer to get projects done. However, if you do not want to borrow money or get into too much debt, this may be a good option.

- **Use a credit card promotion** — Some promotions offer no payments and no interest for six months or longer. Borrow now and pay the credit card balance off within the designated time period. If you cannot pay off the card within the allotted time, keep in mind that the interest rates will be high after the promotional period ends. It is best not to take this approach unless you can pay off the total amount before the interest begins accruing.

- **Get a home equity loan** — This type of loan pays out the money in a lump sum. The amount of equity (or collateral) in the home is the amount that can be borrowed. Improvement projects can increase the value of a home, and most lenders offer home equity loans. Most home equity loans offer a variable interest rate, so be cautious that the rate does not go too high during the duration of the loan. Some lenders offer a fixed rate, but it is usually higher than the variable rate. These types of loans are usually paid off in 15 years, but the payoff could range between five to 30 years. Like any mortgage, you need to find the best interest rates and lowest closing costs available at the time the application is made. Before applying, figure out how to re-pay the home equity loan.

- **Get a home equity line of credit** — The home equity line of credit is a version of revolving credit, with the home acting as collateral. The lender determines an amount as a line of credit, and money is withdrawn from the credit line, as needed. Typically, this amount is determined by subtracting the balance due on the primary mortgage from a percentage of the appraised value of the home. This works the same as the revolving credit principle of a consumer credit card. For example, if the home equity line of credit is $10,000 and $6,000 is withdrawn, then there is $4,000 left in the account. If $6,000 is paid back to credit account, then the credit limit returns to the original amount of $10,000.

- **Get a second mortgage** — A second mortgage enables a certain amount of money to be repaid over a set amount of time The benefit of a second mortgage over a home equity line of credit is that one can obtain a certain amount of money to pay for the renovation project.

- **Get a construction loan** — This is a loan taken out for construction purposes; these are often obtained for new construction, but they can also be used for additions or major renovations. The borrower usually pays the interest-only on the loan until the work is completed. Each lender will set up the money distribution, but there are periodic reviews of the construction process to make sure the money is being used for construction and not other debts. They are short-term loans, so the homeowner draws money out of the loan as needed to pay workers and suppliers. After the work is completed, a certificate of occupancy is given, and the loan is due in full. If the borrower cannot pay off the construction loan in full, the lender can convert the loan to a traditional mortgage. Ideally, the borrower combines the construction loan with the existing primary mortgage into a "new" first mortgage. Only look at a second mortgage (home equity loan) if the appraisal is not high enough to justify the larger first mortgage.

Approaching lenders

No matter what kind of loan is sought, the best way to approach a lender is the same way they were approached him for the first mortgage. Here are some tips on approaching lenders:

Lenders look at a loan applicant's credit score during the application process. A credit score provides a summary of an individual's credit history for the lender. Lenders view good credit scores as a sign that you are a good candidate to receive a loan. Before you see a lender, make sure to obtain your credit score. Try to enhance it if you are not in good standing. A "good" credit score amounts to about 720 or higher on a scale of 850. This score is used by mortgage lenders to determine who receives what loan and at what interest rate. With a higher score, chances increase to receive a loan with an attractive interest rate.

A bad score (about 450 or less) will prolong the loan process. Equifax, TransUnion, and Experian are three companies that keep credit scores on hand. By federal law, consumers can obtain a free credit report every year from each company. The Annual

To improve your score, try these tips:

1. Pay bills on time. Creditors like consistency.

2. Keep overall debt at a reasonable ratio to income. Pay off debt.

3. Use credit cards responsibly.

4. Do not consolidate credit card accounts to one or two cards. Keeping a low balance on several credit cards is better than keeping a high balance on a few.

5. Do not close out your old credit card accounts. Part of the score is based on history, the age of your oldest account, and the average age of your accounts.

6. Make sure you periodically use all your cards. Pay the bill in full when due.

Credit Report's official Web site is **www.annualcreditreport.com**. Before applying for a loan, get a credit report and improve upon any errors so you can present your best image to lenders. Negative credit information is kept for seven years, and lenders might look at more recent, positive activity.

The number of years for a mortgage influences the monthly payment. Most loans are written for 15 to 30 years, and your monthly payments are higher when the number of years you get the mortgage for are lower. Sometimes the lender will require you to pay your interest and taxes in your monthly payment, rather than counting on you to pay them on your own. If refinancing, do not forget closing costs. These are the expenses buyers and sellers experience when changing the ownership of a property. Closing costs can include lender fees, title charges, government recording fees, escrow, and pre-paid items. Sometimes closing costs are used as negotiating points between buyers and sellers. These costs need to be paid up-front at the time of the closing and can cost upward of $3,000. Bankrate, Inc. is an online financial publishing Web site that includes a ranking list of closing costs by state. Visit **www.bankrate.com** to see what the average closing costs will be for your state; click on the "News & Advice" link.

Getting a loan is based on statistics and numbers, and the ability to make the monthly payment on a loan is based on income. Lenders determine an applicants' income and want to know how long they have been at their present job — being on the job for two to three years is considered a solid employment situation. They are also interested in knowing how stable employment is for the future. Lenders can also look at other sources of income in determining eligibility, such as rental incomes, pensions, and investment tools.

The lender looks at outstanding debts and monthly financial obligations. Finally, the debt-to-equity ratio is another number lenders look at in determining the viability of an application.

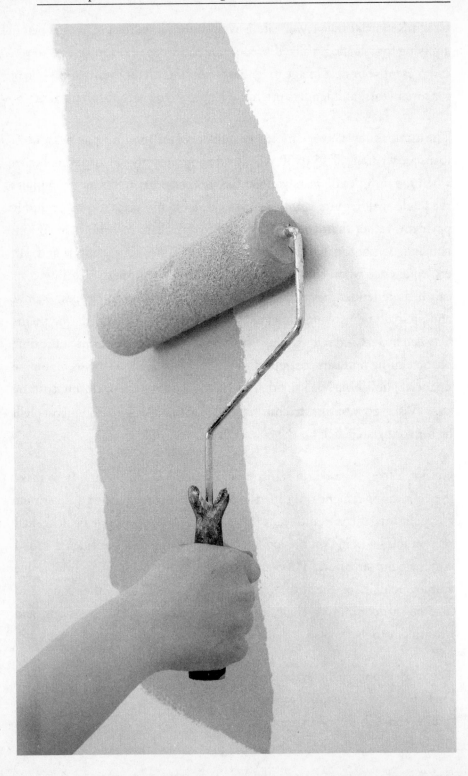

CHAPTER 5

Working Up from the Bottom

If the foundation or frame of the home has problems, they need to be resolved before beginning any other projects. The foundation is the main support to your house. If the foundation has structure problems, all other projects will be affected. The frame and the roof are other high-priority repairs or replacements that should be handled first. As much as you want to start on a new kitchen or paint the dining room, it is wise to make sure the house is plumb, square, level, and dry first. Sure, it is fine to dream about the master bedroom's bathroom renovation, the expansion of the family room, or the new garage workshop — but first things first.

When you walk through the house, look for:

- Cracks in vertical walls wider than ⅛ inch
- Cracks with differential settling of wall sections on either side of the crack
- Cracks that show recent or continuous movement
- Previously repaired cracks
- Cracks on painted surfaces with no paint in cracks
- Cracks with newer, sharp edges
- Caving or bulging of foundation walls

- Corner or center uplift on each side of foundation
- Major cracks (larger than 1 inch wide) in the foundation
- Sloping floors
- Shaky stairways
- Doors that do not close because frames are uneven
- Gaping joints

Foundations

The foundation is the most important part of a house. As it settles or moves on its "footings," so does the house. Failed foundations can lead to moisture problems and water entering the house. Uneven settlements can distort the house frame or pull the house apart. When various forces affect the house foundation, such as weather or insect damage, the foundation is susceptible to failure. Cracks in the concrete footings can lead to a collapse of an entire building. Gravity, soil swelling, and frost heaving are the forces that can damage footings and foundations.

The movement from the expansion and contraction of the soil can cause footer and foundation damage. One solution is to keep the soil around the footprint of the house moist, not soaked or dried out. It is the extreme conditions of the soil that can cause the failure. If the footer sits on hard and compacted soil, it will have a better chance of lasting many years — better yet, a lifetime. Foundation soundness is essential for any additional renovations to the house. All other repairs will be based on the soundness of the foundation.

Foundation repairs

Repairs to foundations can be costly. The costs to repair a moderate foundation problem can run between $8,000 and $30,000, depending on the severity of the problem. Homeowners' insurance will not cover these types of repairs. The following are cost estimates for foundation repairs:

Foundation costs:

- A civil engineer's inspection and report costs between $300 and $800.

- An engineer who specializes in geologic problems can run soil tests and an analysis. The report costs between $500 and $2,000.

- The cost to repair a crack for a poured concrete slab foundation is between $400 and $800.

- The cost to replace a basement concrete floor is between $600 and $1,200.

- The cost to install piers made out of concrete or steel is between $1,000 and $3,000 for each pier.

Figure that piers will need to be placed from 6 to 8 feet apart. Replacing piers in the corner of a house can cost between $3,500 and $5,000. Soil creates many of the foundation problems, so each project will depend on how poor the soil is and how deeply the new piers need to be placed.

If the house is an investment property, then the cost to repair the foundation minimizes or depletes any profit. If you have not purchased the house yet, get a structural engineer to conduct an evaluation. Make your decision to buy the property after receiving the estimate; foundations are a deal-maker or deal-breaker. If the estimate on repairing the foundation is high but the house has other redeeming qualities that make taking on these repairs worthwhile, then proceed to buy the house. If you already live in the house and love living there, then fix the problem.

Many foundation specialty companies charge double per cubic yard for a major repair job versus what they would charge for pouring a new foundation. Unfortunately, problems are likely to occur once the foundation work begins, and estimates are not firm, which means the cost might grow before the work is completed. If the foundation has major problems and you are a novice at renovating, then a professional should evaluate your house to confirm and fix the solution.

Anatomy and inspection

Materials used to make footings are a vast improvement from what they were 100 years ago. Materials and building expertise have become more durable through technological advances. For example, in older homes, stone foundations are not as strong as brick, block, or concrete; they are not the best as load-bearing material.

The foundation walls need to be high enough to direct water away from a house. These walls should be 8 feet above the finish grade to protect the house from soil and moisture. If the house has a basement, then the finished basement walls should provide 7 feet, 4 inches of headspace. Crawl spaces should be 18 inches high to allow for an inspection. Building codes have changed over the years, but there are still many homes built on posts or piers that are worth renovating. If the house has a basement, inspecting the foundation will be easier. The inspection will reveal the original structure, floor plan, and any remodeling alterations. Remodeling is not always as well done as original construction. The date and where the work was done will tell some of the story:

- **Example 1** — If a house were built in a neighborhood that experienced a decline in the real estate values due to an economic depression, then most of the renovations might have been made in a "quick-and-dirty" fashion. This is when builders use shortcuts to cut costs. For example, after the stock market crash of 1929, many in the United States were in financial ruin. This is a time period in which home renovations would have to be done in an inexpensive fashion among many citizens. Additionally, a real estate decline began in 2007 and is still leveling off. This may continue to affect prices of older homes.

- **Example 2** — If wealthy homeowners remodeled their house in an up-and-coming neighborhood, then the work may be of better quality. This would have been especially true if they bought the house to live in.

While in the basement, look at the following:

- **Sills, the main supporting beams, and the posts that hold them up** — You will know whether these structures are sound if they are solid. An ice pick is a good tool to probe wood where there are indications of rot. The exterior face and the underside are prime locations. Using the ice pick, you should be able to hit solid wood within half an inch. Soft spots are an indication of rot from insects or moisture.

- **Joists, girders, and the undersides of floorboards** — If any of these wood members are rotted, they will need to be replaced. Use the same ice pick method to test for rot. If any wood is crumbling, is splitting, is hollow, or has soft spots when the ice pick is used, it will need to be replaced. If the wood is solid, sound, and able to support the house, then proceed to the rest of the inspection. Replacing the joists, subflooring, cellar posts, and floorboards increases the cost but is not prohibitive.

- **In historic homes, the overarching goal is to replace the least amount of original materials as possible** — "Repair instead of replace" is the mantra. For example, if a piece of wood in the basement is rotting but still has some life left in it, then use epoxies and resin compounds to fill and repair the weak areas. These repair products are the preferred approach to fixing the problem instead of replacing the entire piece of wood, especially with a historic house. They will work well when only a section of the wood is rotted and there is still some hard wood present.

For example, the Protective Coating Company in Allentown, Pennsylvania, manufactures a line of products made specifically for wood preservation and restoration. They offer three main solutions to treat damaged wood. First, they have a treatment to kill and prevent infestations of decay fungi. It also helps to kill and prevent an infestation of wood destroying insects. It can be used on both old and new wood.

Another product is an epoxy-based consolidator that hardens and strengthens rotted and damaged wood that has been exposed to insects, water, and UV sunlight. Finally, they have an epoxy paste that replaces and rebuilds missing and rotted wood. All resources are suitable for interior and exterior wood in older and historic homes. To learn more about their products, visit their Web site at **www.pcepoxy.com**.

- **Assess condition of bulkheads and cellar windows, and determine damages** — Replacing windows and bulkheads can be a manageable repair, depending on the severity of the damage.

Settlement

Soil, moisture, and seasonal wetness and dryness can change the bearing capacity of the soil. Wet soil and frost heaves increase pressure against the foundation walls and cause them to bulge. Severe droughts cause soil to dry and shrink, which can also have an adverse impact on a foundation. If a house has excessive settlement, it is advisable to contact a professional for an evaluation of the damage.

Fixing serious foundation problems and beefing up the foundation will support other projects a home needs. Unless you are experienced and confident in your ability to handle foundation problems, it is best to hire a professional who has the proper equipment and experience to resolve these repairs.

Fixing a hairline crack

When the footings of a home are unevenly loaded, normal settlement occurs. The footings might rest on soil that has a bearing capacity not uniform along the lengths of the footings. Foundations adjust to natural forces in the first few years after construction. Minor hairline cracks that are stable are not a problem and do not need to be addressed, but they should be watched for further deterioration and widening. A good method to determine if a crack is active is to mark each end with a pencil; check back on a monthly basis to see if the crack has grown.

The following cracks need to be monitored to prevent deterioration:

- Any cracks wider than ⅛ inch
- Any cracks that look active
- Cracks that were previously repaired and have begun to open up
- Cracks on a painted surface that show no paint in the crack
- Any cracks with a newer and sharper edge

Fixing an active hairline crack in the foundation is fairly simple and a reasonable do-it-yourself project. This technique is meant to fix cracks that are 1 inch or less. A routing-and-sealing method can easily solve the problem. First, widen the crack to about ¼-inch wide and deep with either a chisel and hammer or a concrete saw. After routing the crack, make sure the valley is clean of any little bits of leftover concrete. Clean with a shop vacuum or a fine-bristle brush. Fill the space with an elastic sealant that remains flexible for expansion and contraction of the concrete.

Insect control

Wood-loving insects can damage wood if conditions are right for them to live and thrive in a house. Termites, carpenter ants, and powder-post beetles — insects that might be in the wood when it is installed — do their best work after the wood is installed. Other insects enjoy the nourishment of standing or recently felled trees. If damaged wood is seen in the foundation and you are suspicious of insects, have an exterminator come inspect. Treat the home if necessary, then fix the damaged wood. Get an annual inspection by the exterminator to make sure there is no further infestation.

Frames

The frame of your house is the second-most important in your structural systems. The frame is the main connector between the foundation, roof, walls, doors, windows, electrical and plumbing systems, floors, ceilings, light fixtures, and cabinetry. Many old houses have sagging floors and walls that tilt, but it is possible to improve these imperfections by making them square, plumb, and level. This involves using new materials and structures to align and support the old with the new materials.

Older homes in the United States have three standard styles of frame construction:

1. **Timber frames** — Earliest colonial period; around early 1600s until the end of the 18th century
2. **Balloon frames** — 1832 until World War II (1940)
3. **Platform frames** — Post-World War II

No matter what type of frame your house has, moisture makes wood rot. The most vulnerable area susceptible to rot is the sill, which is the wood that rests on the foundation. Water is prone to get trapped in the space between the sill and the top of the foundation walls, or the back of the sheathing boards. Water from condensation will run down the vertical members of a window and pool on top of the sills when walls are not properly insulated. Old wood, which is continually exposed to moisture, will rot sooner than new wood because their natural wood-preserving resins have weakened with time. Dry wood will remain in good shape over the years.

CHAPTER 6

From the Top to Bottom and the Outside to the Inside

Roofs

The roof is next on the list of priorities in renovating the exterior structures of your home. The roof protects your home from the outdoors: wind, rain, sun, animals, and other elements of nature. Prior to beginning interior projects, fix any roofing problems by repairing or replacing the existing structure. Once the roof is sufficiently repaired or replaced, move on to interior renovations.

A new roof usually increases the value of any property. If you plan to live in the house, you get to enjoy the benefits of a solid roof system, and if you plan to sell the house, you add a positive selling point to the property. This is a win-win renovation.

Standard styles of roofs

The standard styles of roofs found on many older homes are the following:

- **Gable or pitched roof** — A gable roof is a triangular roof, which has a straight slope falling from ridge to eave, creating a peak or triangle on the side or front of the house. The gable roof allows rain and snow to run off easily.

- **Dormer** — A dormer is a window that is vertically set on a sloping roof, and the dormer has its own roof.

- **Hip roof** — This style slopes down to the eaves on all four sides of the house.

- **Cross-hipped** — Similar to a hip roof, but this roof has two parts that cross.

- **Mansard roof (sometimes called a French roof)** — This roof has two different roof pitches. The top pitch is lower-sloped, and the bottom pitch is steep and often has dormers set in it.

- **Gambrel roof** — This roof is two-sided, with a double pitch on each side. This type of roof appears on many hay barns found in rural America. The lower slope has a deeper tilt than the upper slope.

- **Saltbox** — This is a sloping gable roof that usually is found on a saltbox house. It gets its name and design from the box that is used to store salt. It is asymmetrical in that the roof accommodates a house that is typically two stories in the front that slopes in the rear to a one or one-and-a-half-story house.

- **A-frame** — The A-frame provides both the roof and the walls. Originally it was used for cottages, but it can found on a home or church and is often seen in ski resort areas.

- **Flat roof** — A flat roof is actually its own type of roof style. It is also called a low-slope roof and is almost completely horizontal. To prevent water from pooling on this type of flat surface, the roof will have a slight slope so water can roll off. The flat roof is prevalent in dry climates, and it is an easy style of roof to build, requiring few materials.

Roofing materials

There are several materials used for a roof, but not every material is suited for every style. It is best to replace a roof with the existing material, but this might not be the case if the current roof is not the best for the house. This will be dependent on several factors:

- Are you trying to restore the house back to its original state?
- When was the current roof put on?
- How many roofs has the house had?
- Was the original roof metal?
- Would you like to return to the original roof material?
- If the roof is asbestos shingle, should it be replaced with slate or tile?

Be sure the house structure can sustain the additional weight of one of these heavier materials. There is no harm in exploring the alternatives. Some materials do better in certain climates and regions of the United States.

Main types of materials used for roofs:

MATERIAL	ANTICIPATED LIFESPAN	BEST CLIMATE TO USE IT IN
Wood shingles	30 to 40 years	Some building codes require roofing materials to be fireproof; there might not be an alternative
Wood shakes	30 to 40 years	Some building codes require roofing materials to be fireproof; these might not be an alternative
Asphalt shingles	20 years	Everywhere
Slates	80 years	New England
Asbestos cement shingles	30 to 50 years	Everywhere (no longer manufactured); replaced with cement-fiber shingles in the 1970s

Ceramic or clay tiles	50 years	Warmer climates, such as California, Arizona, Texas, New Mexico, and Florida
Built-up, 3-ply for flat roofs	15 to 20 years	Everywhere
Built-up, 4-ply for flat roofs	20 to 25 years	Everywhere
Metal – today, most are galvanized metal	40 to 50 years	New England, the Southern states

The roof system

The roof system is composed of several parts that make up the whole:

- **Rafters** — These are the sloping beams that support the weight load of the roof. They run from the top of the roof's ridgeline to the eaves. They form the framework or skeleton of the roof, and part of the roof truss.

- **Sheathing or decking** — On a shingle roof are these plywood, particleboard, or water wafer board panels that are used to cover the rafters. The roofing material is attached to this sheathing.

- **Ridge boards** — This is the highest point of the roof that encompasses the span of the roof.

- **Hip** — The outer angle created by the intersection of two slanted roof planes.

- **Collar beams** — This is a beam that connects rafters from opposite sides of the roof together. It keeps the roof from spreading apart.

- **Roof trusses (more common today)** — The framework of beams that support the roof.

- **Valley** — An inner angle created by the intersection of two slanted roof planes.

- **Dormers** — These elevate from the roof and are often apart from the roof-to-wall junction.

- **Underlay or tar paper** — Providing an extra layer of protection from moisture, this is heavy felt paper put on top of decking prior to the installation of roofing material.

- **Flashing** — These are pieces of metal used to prevent water from coming in through any intersection or projection in a roof and the vertical walls. Examples of where flashing is required are in vent pipes, dormers, chimneys, valleys, and the joints at vertical walls. Water from rain, snow, and ice can leak into the house through the valleys and damage the walls and wood. The metal is sold in rolls and can be cut to size. Because it is dangerous to work with, wear gloves, long sleeves, and pants — no shorts.

- **Fascia** — This is trim used to enclose the shaft end of the rim. It is often found where gutters are joined to the house.

- **Soffit** — This is the completed underside of the rim. Resembling a small ceiling, it encompasses the area between the tip of the rim and the underside of a roof overhang.

- **Turret** — This is a small tower that protrudes sideways from the wall of a building. They were used as a military defense mechanism in medieval castles.

Determine whether a roof needs to be repaired or replaced by taking a close look. In some instances, you will need to walk on the roof to check the condition. This is the time to decide if you want to have a professional handle the job. To conduct a preliminary evaluation and determine any deterioration on the roof, use the following checklist:

OBSERVATIONS	YES	NO	NOT SURE OR N/A
Does the roof have leaks?			
Are walls or ceilings blistered?			
Are there dark rings on the ceilings?			
Does the roof have streaks?			
Are shingles missing?			
Is the roof wavy or sagging in spots?			
Are the soffits sagging?			
Asphalt shingles: Are they curling, brittle, or tearing?			
Wooden shingles: Is there dry rot or are they warped?			
Metal roofs: Are there signs of pitting, rusting, corrosion, loose or open seams, and joints that can result in leaking?			
Slate roofs: Are slates missing, broken, or about to fall off?			
Is there damage to the flashings?			
Do you see any damage under eaves and overhangs that indicate water leakage, especially near dormers or skylights?			

Fixing minor roof repairs

If you attempt to fix minor repairs, be sure you are able to climb a ladder and get on the roof. It is a good idea to have someone with you in case you need a hand. Wear shoes and clothing that are appropriate for this project. Avoid repairs when the weather is very hot or cold. If you are using tar or caulk, follow the manufacturer's directions for temperature and product effectiveness.

- To prevent further damage, fix roof leaks as soon as you notice them.

- If you are able to go into the attic, search for water damage underneath the roof deck. You will get the best idea of where repairs are necessary.

- Tar can halt leakage on an asphalt shingle roof.

- To avoid wrecking the shingle, try to twist the nails off the damaged shingle carefully.

- For repair work, it is not easy to match shingles. Lift the tabs and place a coat of tar underneath the tear. If in good condition, use the original nails to nail the shingle to the deck using a hammer. New roof nails can be used if necessary.

- When using tar, apply a heavy coat over the tear and spot over each nail head.

- If constructing new nail holes, place a spot of tar on both the old and new nail holes.

- To avoid ice from forming under the shingle in the winter, place another thin line of tar underneath the shingles to overlap the damages.

- Be sure to place extra tar underneath the new shingle in the event that the seal may have been broken when lifting for repair work.

- Use caution when working with older shingles. They may contain asbestos, and if they are brittle and crack when you are working with them, they can release asbestos fibers into the air. *See Chapter 2 for more information on asbestos and how to handle it.*

Leaks

If there are more leaks near the chimney or vents, this usually means there is a gap where the chimney or vent meets the flashing. This can be the result of caulk or tar drying out and cracking, which results in the gap.

How to resolve a leak

Usually a good, thick bead of tar will fix the leak. If this does not work, the flashing might need to be replaced. This can be accomplished with a roll or two of aluminum flashing, tar, and roofing nails.

1. Using a pair of tin snips, cut replacement pieces of flashing.

2. Gently remove or loosen shingles and remove old flashing; tar around the edges of where the damage is located.

3. Place the new flashing down with roofing nails; make sure it butts up against the chimney or vent.

4. Apply a thick coat of tar to seal the edges and replace the original shingles back in place.

Roofing cement is a product used to fix minor cracks, to fill holes, or patch damages. Roof patch products come in 1-gallon (or larger) cans or buckets; for small cracks and imperfections, repair products come in easy-to-use caulk tubes. Other problems to address prior to beginning interior renovations are: sagging ridge boards, rafters, and roof sheathing.

Replacing a roof

If you need to replace a roof, there are several factors to determine the cost:

• **Materials** — Not every material is suitable for every roof. Flat roofs need a different material than sloped roofs. Costs of materials vary.

• **The size of roof needs to be determined in order to purchase supplies** — Roofers talk in squares, not square feet. One square = 100 square feet in area or a 10- by 10-foot square. Example: A 2,000-square-foot house with a gable roof equals less than 1,500 square feet of roofing area, or approximately 15 squares.

- **Shape of roof** — The simpler the style of the roof, the simpler it will be to replace it. The more intersecting rooflines (valleys), chimneys, turrets, skylights, vent pipes, dormers, or other elements in a roof, the higher the replacement costs. If the peak of the roofline is steep, it will be more expensive to replace.

- **Condition of existing roof** — Does the existing roof need to be removed, or can the new roof be placed over the present one? If the existing roof needs to be removed, this can add to the cost.

  Is the sheathing (or decking) in good shape, or does it need to be repaired or replaced? This will influence the cost.

- **Hammer or nail gun** — This is a personal choice. The job is faster with a nail gun, but some prefer a hammer. Nail gunners require a compressor, and if not owned already, they can both be purchased.

Metal roofing has made a comeback over the last few years. If you have an asbestos shingle roof and you do not want to remove the old shingles, it is possible to put a metal roof over the shingles. A professional roofer can determine if this is feasible. The other consideration is whether a metal roof fits the style of the house. Look at other houses in the area to see if any similar to yours have a metal roof; see if you like it.

A general rule of thumb is that if there are two asphalt shingle roofs in place, do not add a third layer of shingles to the roof. The shingles will not lie down properly. Weight is another consideration. If there are foundation problems on the house, then even two roofs can be an issue. Consult a roofer and foundation expert before adding more weight to the roof with a second roof.

Problems with valleys in a roof can be the culprit behind many roof leaks. If you hire a roofing company, make sure they replace the existing flashing material and not just use tar to repair valleys. This type of shortcut can create leaks later on. If you are intimidated by the prospect of putting on a new roof yourself, then call in a reputable roofing contractor.

CASE STUDY: A PROFESSIONAL ROOFER'S ADVICE

Bill Chafin
Roofer
Huntington, West Virginia
billchafin@aol.com

Know what it is involved in putting on a new roof before taking off the old one. "Most homeowners are better off not putting on their own roofs," said Bill Chafin, a roofer for more than 25 years. The biggest demand is the physical exertion on the body. "Most people are just not physically capable of carrying the weight of a bundle of shingles." The second requirement is to be able to climb up and down ladders several hours a day. "It is a workout from daylight to dark, and even some athletes in Gold's Gym couldn't handle it," Chafin said.

A bundle of shingles used to weigh 72 pounds and came with a 20-year guarantee. Today, bundles weigh 92 pounds and have a 25-, 30-, 35-, or even a 50-year guarantee. Remember, the longer the guarantee, the heavier the shingle. Also come prepared, Chafin said.

"There is the need to be agile and to always be able to remember where your feet are going to next while on the roof so you will not slip. A roofer needs to be light on their toes and have the ability to feel where they are walking. It is good to wear heavy boots, but not boots with very thick soles. You will not be able to feel the roof under your feet."

"There is a great deal of planning that goes on with roof work. Looking at a job and how a roof is designed will help to plan the job," Chafin said.

To replace decking, use plywood or USB board. Plywood is measured in squares, where one sheet of plywood is 4 by 8 feet, or 32 square feet. Three sheets of plywood amount to 96 square feet, so one bundle of shingles encompasses three sheets of plywood.

"The other key material is the roof felt, which comes in 15-pound rolls; two squares will cover this amount of felt. Four squares will cover a 30-

pound roll of felt," Chafin said. Nails can be banged in with a hammer or with a pneumatic nail gun, which makes the job go quicker.

Weather plays a big part. A roofer can work on sections of a roof to prevent the weather from having a negative impact on the project. Once a roof has been removed, the interior of the house is in a vulnerable state, and the roofer needs to be vigilant about weather conditions.

Chafin said he plans ahead for the day and week according to weather. "Weather has such a big impact on putting on a roof that I need to stay one step ahead of it to keep the inside of a house dry," Chafin said. "When putting on a roof, you need to think about water constantly and how it drains. This will result in putting on the roof so there will be no leaks."

All components on a roof overlap. One cannot predict what will be found once the old roof is removed. "There might be structural damage in the rafters, all or part of the decking might need replacing, or other repairs might have to be done before I can put the new shingles on," Chafin said. Once the old shingles come, be prepared to handle what is below. Putting on a roof is not for the faint of heart.

"There is also a trick to cutting shingles," Chafin said. "I use a hook knife (which is a utility knife with hook blades) to trim shingles to fit." By puncturing the middle of the shingle and pulling the knife down to cut, Chafin said, cutting the other portion off is much more simple. "All these tricks lead to saving money on materials."

Chafin recommends keeping the work site clean to avoid stepping on nails or brads that have fallen around the work site. Additionally, he says to keep a cover over all materials to deter thieves and prevent moisture from building up. Finally, Chafin offers this suggestion: "If a homeowner really wants to put on their own roof, make sure they have someone experienced in roofing running the job. There needs to be a lead person in charge of the project, and if there is a friend or family member [who] is experienced, then approach them to run the job to prevent problems mid-stream." Most roofs need replacing because they leak.

Gutters

Gutters provide a critical role to your home's well-being. Without gutters, you invite water problems in the basement, foundation, exterior and interior walls, and your landscaping materials. If they are not sufficient in size, there are not enough downspouts, or they do not direct the water away from the property, then they are virtually useless. Take a good look at your gutters and how they perform on a rainy day. If they are overflowing, leaking, causing water to run down the side of your house, or being surrounded by pools of water around the foundation, then they are not properly functioning.

Maintenance is key with gutters. Conduct a biannual inspection in the late spring and late fall. If you clean your own gutters, be sure to have a sturdy exterior extension ladder to stand on. To clean them, begin by clearing debris and checking for obstructions that would prevent the steady flow of water. After you clean the larger pieces of debris, use a garden hose to clean the gutters and wash away dirt or smaller debris. While you have the garden hose, run water and see how well the gutters are functioning. If you still see overflowing, then it might mean you do not have enough downspouts to handle the volume of water.

There are many styles of gutters on the market, made of different materials. Much of the decision-making comes down to price and appearance. Typically, there are more problems with gutters in colder climates due to ice jams and debris from fall foliage. These jams block the flow of water, and the weight of ice and snow on the gutter weakens their performance. In some cold and wet areas such as Vermont, homeowners frustrated with gutters that break often opt to not replace damaged gutters.

Gutter materials

Gutters are made of the following materials:

MATERIAL	PROS	CONS	PRICE
Wood	Ideal for restorations of older homes; attractive and suits some styles of homes perfectly.	Expensive, needs maintenance, and less performance because wood slows down water flow. Difficult to find.	$12 to $20 per linear foot.
Copper	Attractive, great for restorations and looks nice on certain styles of homes. Minimal maintenance: Does not rust; does not need painting.	Expensive.	$15 per linear foot.
Aluminum	Does not rust, inexpensive, comes in many colors. Pre-finished aluminum gutters have a baked-on enamel finish — this makes them immune to corrosion.	Seamless gutters are the best because non-seamless gutters can leak. However, it is more expensive because it is a custom job.	$5 to $9 per linear foot.
Vinyl	Will not rust or rot. Inexpensive. Easy to install yourself with their snap-together sections and couplings.	Can break down. Will get brittle when exposed to cold of winter and heat of summer. Will need periodic replacement, and only come in brown or white.	Sold in 10-foot lengths at $3 to $5.
Galvanized steel	Least expensive, sturdier than aluminum, and comes in many colors. Half-round gutters are suitable for older homes vs. aluminum or vinyl.	Will rust; needs to be painted periodically; sections need to be soldered together. If rusty spots are repaired with a metal patch right away, they will last longer.	$4 to $8 per linear foot.

Although you will still find wooden gutters on some of the older homes, they are not found often. In the 1960s, aluminum and vinyl gutters first appeared and monopolized the marketplace. Copper has begun to make a comeback by those with historic houses and those interested in replacing original materials with other original materials. Copper gutters have a classic look with a longer life expectancy than other metal gutters. Although more expensive, they are a suitable replacement gutter and help to restore the original look of an older or historic home.

A few tips to remember:

- Gutters are sold by the thickness of the material they are made of. The thicker gutters will hold up to weather and elements. They run in gauges from 0.19 to 0.32 inches thick, with the thickest being the most expensive.

- Gutters are either seamless or come in sections. Seamless gutters will not leak, but sectional systems can leak. Professionals are the only ones who install the seamless variety because specific equipment is required. Homeowners will not want to make the costly investment in this type of equipment. It makes more sense to have a professional install them.

- Make sure the downspouts run into a proper drainage system.

- If you hire a contractor, be sure to obtain references. The gutter installation business is a fairly inexpensive type of business to start, so there are many unreliable companies that open quickly and close just as fast. It is best to hire a reputable company that has been in business for a while.

- The main point to remember when you replace gutters or repair them is to make sure the gutters keep water away from the house.

From the Outside In: Exterior Trim and Siding

Now that the main structural projects are completed and your house is in good shape as far as the foundation, frame, and roof goes, it is time to decide if you want to begin work on the exterior of the house or tackle the interior projects. This is not always a clear-cut call because other factors will influence your decision. For instance, who will be doing the work?

If you are hiring a professional, then their availability becomes a factor. The nature of the repairs and the weather will dictate the best time of the year to complete the project. If you are painting the house, product labels will offer guidelines and a temperature range as to when you will achieve the best results. If you are repairing mortar on a brick house, then you will not be doing this work in the middle of winter in upstate New York, but you might be able to do it in Georgia. If you prefer to start on the outside and all variables line up in your favor, then the next logical project to plan is the renovation of the exterior trim and siding.

Repairing and replacing the siding and trim on your older home is the last of the fundamental exterior projects. Later on in the book, we head back outdoors and discuss porches, decks, landscaping, and garages. Depending on your skills as a painter and a carpenter, and the size and scope of the project, you might do this project yourself. On the other hand, you might call in a contractor or subcontractor to handle one or both of these tasks. The extent of these renovations is dependent on the condition of the exterior siding and trim of your home.

If you have a masonry surface on the exterior of your home, you will find that the most common repairs are to fix cracks, replace missing mortar, and repair or replace eroded stones or bricks. Fixing the foundation first might have created some additional repair projects for the exterior, but at least now you are on a solid footing to successfully restore the rest of your home.

Brick and stone repair

Common problems with brick and stone houses are cracks, stains, crumbling mortar, and erosion of the brick or stone. Depending on the severity of the damages, there are many repairs that can be done to replace the mortar, stone, or brick, and to clean the surface properly.

Re-pointing

Re-pointing is the mason's term for the process of replacing a mortar joint when the mortar is cracked, broken, or loose. If the whole house, from top to bottom, needs re-pointing, this requires more extensive repairs. Calling in a professional mason for a consultation or a quote before attempting the project yourself is best. If you do want to consult with a mason, it is important to work with one who is experienced in doing masonry work on older homes. Today's brick homes are different than the ones constructed a century or two ago, especially when it comes to the materials. Homes built before the 1920s have bricks and mortar that are softer than the bricks and mortar used today.

There are nuances to re-pointing brick and stone, and finding or creating the right replacement mortar is the key to a successful project. Many of the older homes were built in the days when there was no cement and the mortar was made primarily of lime and sand. Trying to replace mortar on your older home with all-modern cement will not work. Cement is too hard, becomes brittle, and will only last for a few years. There are some tried-and-true methods to determine what the mortar should be composed of.

Mortar

Knowing the age of the home and its renovation history will give the first clue as to the composition of the mortar originally used to point the bricks. Try to match the color and texture of either the original mortar or the mortar used in earlier repairs. Older mortar was made primarily from lime, sand, and water. This mixture was conducive to the expansion and contraction of bricks during different temperatures and allowed moisture to evaporate.

Today's Portland cement does not have the elasticity of lime and will not move with the brick, will not allow moisture to evaporate, and becomes hard and brittle. There may be sections of the house that reveal attempts to repair brick joints with the wrong mortar. These sections can be fixed with a fairly simple tuck-pointing project, described in this next section.

TIME PERIOD	COMPOSITION OF MORTAR
Antique mortar	2.5 to 3 parts sand to 1 part lime; add a bit of Portland cement to help it cure quicker.
Early industrial to mid-19th century	10 to 12 parts sand, 3 parts lime, and 1 part Portland cement.
Turn of the 20th century to present day	6 to 7 parts sand, 1 part lime, and 1 part Portland cement.

Tuck-pointing

Tuck-pointing is a mason's technique used to replace the cracked, missing, or damaged mortar between bricks. Professional masons make this skill look difficult because they are good at it and move very quickly. The technique can be learned, but it takes time to pick up speed and neatness.

Below are some pointers to tuck-pointing. This type of work requires finesse, time, and patience:

- **Equipment needed:**
    - Safety glasses
    - Cold chisel
    - Heavy hammer
    - Proper mortar
    - A joint tool
    - Mason's trowel
    - A mason's hawk — a rectangular flat surface with a handle under the surface that is perpendicular and something to hold with one hand; you can also use a plastering or a concrete finishing trowel
    - An old, dry paintbrush (or another type of brush that will fit into joints)
    - A stiff-bristle brush
    - A spray bottle with clean drinking water
    - A bucket of water and old rags for clean up

- Do not do re-pointing on days that are too hot or too cold; the mortar will not cure properly. Clean out the old mortar with a cold chisel and hammer. Be cautious during this step — because pieces of the old of mortar will escape, use safety glasses. Try not to hit the bricks with the chisel, and avoid driving the chisel point toward the brick. This will prevent damage to the bricks. Remove old mortar at least ¾-inch deep, if not deeper.

- Use an old paint brush to brush out small bits of old mortar and dust. Do not attempt to place new mortar over old mortar; this will not work. The old mortar must be removed in order for the mortar to stick.

- The mortar in older homes is soft and usually has less cement than today's brick and stone modern homes. If your house is more than 50 years old, do not to buy a ready-mix mortar. Instead, mix your own batch.

- Some restoration masonry companies have pre-mixed mortar that is more suitable for older or historic home do-it-yourself projects. Virginia Lime Works offers several types of pre-mixed mortar exclusively meant for older homes. Visit their Web site at **www.virginialimeworks.com** to learn more about their products and to find a distributor near you. If you send a sample of your mortar to a company such as U.S. Heritage Group, Inc., they will match it. It will take them four weeks to prepare and ship your custom mortar, so plan ahead. Visit their Web site at **www.usheritage.com** for more information on samples and their other services.

If you attempt to mix your own mortar, here are a few suggestions:

- A wheelbarrow works fine. If you are patching a small repair, then a big basin, preferably with a flat bottom, or old piece of clean plywood is sufficient.

- There are a few types of mortar you can buy. Hydraulic lime solid mixes with water. The mortar needs to be the consistency of pudding or mashed potatoes. It should be firm enough to not run when put in the joints, but not too hard, dry, or stiff.

- Purchase lime putty mortar, which comes in buckets pre-mixed.

- Spray the clean joint with a mist of water. The brick and mortar are dry and will soak up this moisture to adhere better. The hawk holds the mortar and rests just below the joint; it acts as a ledge to keep mortar off bricks. It is important to keep mortar off bricks because bricks are difficult to clean. Put some mortar on the pointing trowel and tuck the mortar into the point being filled. Remove excess mortar and pack what remains down with the trowel. It is best if you put the mortar on in steps rather than put all the mortar in the joint in one pass. This makes it easier, but also helps the mortar repair be more successful as it cures. Keep your bucket of fresh water and rags handy for clean up. Change water as necessary.

- Once the mortar begins to harden, use the joint tool to create a concave valley of mortar to match the other points. Gently spray the area with the water to help it cure properly. Misting the area for two days helps the repaired area properly dry.

- If tuck-pointing a historic home, take the bristled end of the stiff brush and hit the mortar (before it dries) a few times to make the new mortar look distressed — this will make it match the rest of the house.

If you want to clean your stone or brick house, you can do this with a power washer on a low-pressurized water setting around 100 pounds per square inch (psi). Scrub the stone or brick with a stiff, natural-bristle or nylon brush. There are brick and masonry detergents available. Check manufacturer guidelines to be sure it is suitable for your project.

Painting a Wood-Exterior House

If you have a wood-exterior house and it needs painting, then the prep work will be the most time-consuming part of the project. If you are doing this project alone, you need to have confidence in your painting ability to move about and climb up and down ladders. Safety is the priority. If you are not up to job, hire a professional. If you decide to do it yourself, here are a few tips to get you going:

- Scaffolding or staging makes painting a house easier. Moving ladders from section to section is tiring and not as efficient. You can rent scaffolding or staging, and some companies will set it up for you. If your house is a ranch or one-story, then you can create your own scaffolding by using sturdy and well-maintained exterior step and extension ladders. Do not use flimsy interior ladders. Make the investment in two (or more) aluminum or fiberglass ladders suited for this purpose. The extension ladder comes in handy in tight spots, especially when you need to lean it against the house.

  Make sure ladders are sturdy and do not sink into the ground. Staging requires sturdy and straight planks that can hold your weight. If there will be more than one person painting, make sure you consider the total weight. Scaffold-grade planks measuring 2 by 10 feet work fine. Some painters put one plank on top of the other for double planks and double strength. Make sure you feel comfortable with the width of the plank and your ability to work safely. Take breaks, and drink plenty of water to keep from getting dehydrated.

- Use a pressure washer to remove loose paint and clean exterior surfaces for dirt, mold, and debris. If you do not have one, rent one. This step will alleviate part of the scraping work.

- Prune shrubs and trees and remove debris on the ground. Remove lawn furniture, toys, potted plants, and any items near the house to protect against paint splatters.

- Use drop cloths or tarpaulins to cover shrubs, plants, and other landscape materials. Coverings can be moved from plant to plant as you move the ladder or scaffolding. If necessary, tie up plant materials such as trellises to keep them safe and out of your way.

- Make sure there are no exposed electrical wires that can be a hazard. Have them properly repaired and covered prior to beginning your project.

- Scraping is tedious and boring, but it is a necessary step, and you will be glad you did it once your paint begins to dry. Your end result will be so much better with the degree of effort you put into the scraping and repairing imperfections on the house. Keep scrapers sharp, wear safety glasses, and wear old but proper clothing to protect against sun, paint, thorns, and branches. It is best to scrape and clean one part of the house and then paint it. This breaks up the monotony of the prep work, and you can see the fruits of your labor.

- One of the biggest hindrances to properly painting a house is the weather. Read your paint labels to determine how long it takes for paint to cure and the recommended temperatures to use the product. Then check the extended weather forecast. Proper weather conditions are vital to having a successful project.

- Choose the correct paint. If your house is painted with latex, use latex; if oil-based, use oil-based. Do not try to put a fresh coat of latex paint on an old coat of oil-based paint; it will not adhere properly. For the amount of work you do on the prep work, the last thing you want to happen is the paint's not adhering properly. It will also not last very long. You do not want to have to paint your house every two years.

- Rub a small section of your house with sandpaper, and if the paint comes off in little balls, it is latex; if it comes off as dusty and chalky, it has an oil base.

- Choosing the color scheme for your house is usually up to you, unless you have a historic house. In this case, the historic commission will offer guidance for colors that would have been used during the period your house was built. In an effort to maintain the historic integrity of the neighborhood, they are required by the federal government to provide this guidance so the neighborhood remains historic in its exterior appearance. If homeowners do not comply, then the district can lose its status as a historic district. Being in one of these neighborhoods usually increases the re-sale value of your home, so it is best to use the appropriate colors. There are numerous resources to help you decide which color works best for your home. No matter what color you choose, it is good to put on a coat of high-quality primer first. This is more expensive and time-consuming, but it will pay off later when the topcoat adheres better and you have to paint less often. If you are changing the color of the house, this primer coat will help to bridge the color gap.

- The decision to use a brush, roller, or spray depends on your house. A 4-inch-wide brush is best for much of the work, but buy some smaller brushes, too. Rollers might work in some sections, but it is better if the house is stucco, stone, or brick.

- When you buy your paint, buy all your supplies and clean-up equipment at the same time. There is nothing worse than having to make several trips to the paint store — that is, unless you want to get away from all the scraping.

CHAPTER 7

Water Systems: Septic Systems, Cesspools, and Water Wells

Having an understanding of the system that supplies water to your house and the system that takes sewage away is important. Urban or suburban dwellers are more likely to have a municipal water supply and a sewer outtake pipe. For the most part, we do not think about these systems unless there is a problem. Unfortunately, municipal water supply sources have challenges in providing clean and safe drinking water. This is leading consumers to install water filtration systems in their homes to address their concerns.

Many rural and suburban dwellers manage their own water supply and wastewater removal systems. Properly maintaining these systems are necessary to keep them running smoothly. Ignoring these systems can lead to costly repairs or replacement. When buying a new home, get as much information about the installation and maintenance of these systems.

Septic Systems

A septic system is responsible for the treatment of household wastewater. It is easy and inexpensive to maintain but expensive to replace. The cost of a new septic system varies according to where it is being placed. One in the Midwest might cost $3,000-$5,000, and one in New Jersey might cost $12,000. It is contingent on labor and material costs in an area and the complexity of the project. Before undertaking the installation of a new system, ask neighbors about the cost to build theirs and for a reference.

Understand how a septic system works and how to keep one running smoothly. Communities, through their building and health codes, usually dictate where tanks and leach fields can be located. Check with localities to determine their regulations. The system comprises four parts. First. a pipe from the house leads to the septic tank. This is how the wastewater leaves the house.

A septic tank is a watertight container, which is basically a holding tank for the wastewater. It is typically made of concrete, fiberglass, or polyethylene. While in the tank, the solids, through gravity, sink to the bottom and develop into sludge. The oils and grease float to the surface and become scum. It is constructed with compartments and a T-shaped outlet that prevents this sludge and scum from leaving the tank.

Eventually, the wastewater does leave the septic tank and seeps into the drain field, which is also known as a leach field. Once the wastewater runs out to the drain field, it permeates into the soil. The final remedy is when the soil discards the harmful bacteria, viruses, and nutrients. Suitable soil is essential for successful wastewater treatment. It is important the soil breaks down waste products and makes them harmless before they reach the groundwater below.

Regular maintenance on a septic system will keep it running smoothly for a long period of time. According to the EPA, 25 percent of U.S. homeowners have septic systems. Proper maintenance saves the homeowner money and protects the health of humans through protecting the environment and drinking water sources. This means homeowners must pump out the septic tank on a regular basis. A regular basis means different schedules for each household. It depends on how much wastewater is running through the system, how many are in the household, and how conservative the occupants are with water usage.

A general rule of thumb is the system should be pumped out at least every three years, if not more often. It is better to err on pumping more often than waiting until the tank is full. Inspect the system for leaks and observe the amount of wastewater in the tank. The tank needs pumping if the scum layer is within 6 inches of the bottom of the outlet tee, or the top of the sludge layer is within inches of the outlet tee.

How to make the septic system last

There are practical tips and habits individuals can adopt to curtail water usage so the septic system will last longer. The key is to conserve water and not overload the amount of wastewater in the tank. Below are some habits, practices, and suggestions on how to keep a septic system functioning properly:

- Keep plumbing fixtures in good order by repairing leaky faucets, running toilets, and any drips.

- Only use dishwashers and washing machines when they are full. Do not run back-to-back loads of laundry or run the dishwasher right after doing a load of laundry (or vice versa).

- Take short showers, and do not flush items such as cat litter, sanitary products, disposable diapers, cigarettes, or paper towels down the toilet.

- Replace older toilets, dishwashers, and washing machines with high-efficiency models; this makes a difference because they use less water so the septic system is not burdened as much by having to process extra water.

- Install faucet aerators, high-efficiency showerheads, and shower flow restrictors to reduce the amount of water being used.

- Do not allow heavy-duty cleaners, strong or hazardous chemicals, fats, oils, and large particles of food to go down the drains.

- It is important that leach fields are not saturated with water; divert water from downspouts away from that area.

- Do not plant trees in the leach field area because roots can damage pipes. Plant dense grasses, shallow root plants, and shrubs to absorb water.

- Do not park vehicles on or drive over the leach field.

- Conduct regular maintenance on the system by pumping out the holding tank according to manufacturer's recommendations. This will typically occur every two to five years based on usage.

- Have a professional do the pumping to avoid gases and bacteria.

Ways to tell if there is a problem with the system

- There is a foul smell in the area of the septic system — a septic system is not doing its job if there is a foul smell in the area. Too much water in the septic tank could be the problem. Check the level of the water in the tank. If the water level is fine, then either the leach field or septic tank has a problem.

- Pools of water or muddy soil are found near the septic system, water drains slowly, gurgling sounds come from drains, or water comes in through the basement or lowest level of the house.

- The toilets back up when flushed. This might happen when you do laundry. You will notice bright green strips of grass over your drain field.

If any of these symptoms occur, contact a professional to check out the system. This is one repair or replacement project you will not want to work on yourself.

A Warning about Septic System Dangers

Decomposing natural waste produces toxic and dangerous gases like methane gas and hydrogen sulfide. Methane is an odorless and colorless flammable gas that, when humans are exposed to it in an enclosed area, can cause asphyxiation or an explosion. Hydrogen sulfide can also be present in the septic tank, where it will create a rotten egg smell. Hydrogen sulfide is also poisonous and flammable. To prevent being overcome by either gas, follow these safety steps:

- Do not ever work alone on a septic system in case there is a problem.
- Do not enter a septic system or lean over into one.
- Do not light a match or flame while in the septic area.
- Do not smoke in the area.
- Make sure the area is well ventilated if doing any work in the septic area.
- Make sure covers are safe and sound so no one can fall in.
- Hire a professional if not confident in your skills to repair or resolve a septic system problem.

Cesspools

The cesspool is another way to remove wastewater from your home. Although the cesspool is a simple and inexpensive installation, it is considered outdated and obsolete by today's standards and has been replaced by the septic system. A cesspool design comprises a large hole in the ground with a rock or concrete-block lining. House sewage runs into this tank, and the liquids trickle through the openings of the lining and the soil soaks it up.

Located at the top of the cesspool is a snug-fitting, concrete lid that shields away insects and vermin. Nearby water supplies and wells can become tainted by this disposal system. Therefore, the contaminated liquids will eventually impact the surrounding earth.

If you have a cesspool, you might consider replacing it with a septic system, if the budget allows. If you have not had any problems with your cesspool, make sure you have it pumped out every two to five years to keep it properly running. Cesspools might be an option in dry climates where there is good drainage and a deep water table.

Water Wells

The majority of Americans get their drinking and household water from a municipality, but according to the National Science Foundation, 20 million Americans get their water from a well. The age of your home does not necessarily determine whether you have "city" water drawn from a municipal source or well water drawn from an on-site well. Even older homes can have city water if they have been in a location where it is available.

Some older homes will have an on-premise well. This water source can be used as a backup or for watering the garden, plants, or washing the car. Monitoring a well's performance will help to keep it running properly and guarantees a safe source of water and money savings.

There are only a few regulations and requirements for homeowners to test their well water for safety and quality. Some localities, however, are beginning to require that wells be tested when the property is sold. If a homeowner wants to test her water, then her local county office usually has resources to help residents perform safety tests. Water can be tested for hardness, pH level, arsenic, radon, and pesticides. Some well water is notorious for having a rotten egg smell, which is a symptom of sulfur in the water. If there is a presence of iron bacteria in the water, there might be a moldy or musty smell.

Red staining of fixtures indicates that the iron levels of the water are not level and the water needs testing. Manganese, a hard and brittle, metal-like chemical element, will cause black or brown staining on laundry. If there are any of these elements discovered after the water is tested, the homeowner can use a water filtration system or a reverse-osmosis system to fix the problem. Annual well water inspections are strongly encouraged.

Wells in the northern part of the United States are usually found in basements, and those in the warmer, southern climates are often found in a pump house. There are some repairs that homeowners can complete on their well system, like replacing a burnt-out pump or a leak. If your well system is old and needs repair, replacing the entire system will be costly, but not prohibitive. Call in a licensed well professional if you need a replacement. Putting in a new well requires several tasks immediately, then some routine tasks over the years.

If you need a new well, hire a local drilling contractor who is experienced and familiar with other wells in the area. Talk with a neighbor for a recommendation. A survey of area wells is necessary before drilling a new well. The survey provides important information about aquifers, water yields, and quality. The contractor will also decide the depth and location of the well, the design, casing material, and seal formation. The contractor will test hole drilling, determine depth, take dirt and rock samples at different depths, and record geologic material found.

Afterward, you and the contractor can identify aquifers with the greatest prospective for water supply. The cost depends on your area and circumstances, but prices average between $3,000 and $4,500. Many homeowners try to delay a total replacement by fixing the leaks as they crop up. A deep well (100 feet) is preferable over a spring. A spring is less reliable and presents limitations in service to the homeowner. The recovery rate for a well should be about 3 gallons per minute. The basic components of a well system are:

- **The pump** — Jet pumps, centrifugal pumps, or rotary pumps.

- **Pressure tank** — It fills and stores water for your use later on. There are simple, single-compartment tanks that hold both air and water. Tanks with an internal bladder use the bladder like a balloon filled with air, which can keep the air and water separate.

- **Water pressure gauge** — The gauge should show 20 pounds per square inch, and preferably between 40 to 50 pounds per square inch. If it is less, then the pump is not working correctly.

Tips for keeping a well working

- Get an inspection to confirm the well is in good working order.

- To find out a system's output, perform a flow test. This will examine the water level before and during pumping.

- Then run a pump-motor performance check, a pressure-tank and pressure-switch contact check, and a general water-quality test.

- Examine the well equipment to ensure it is sanitary and up to local code requirements.

- Check the water for coli-form bacteria and nitrates. Coli-form bacteria can be found in the environment in harmless quantities, but if they are found in drinking water, it might mean these germs can lead to contamination and result in disease. There is also a fecal coli-form bacterium that comes from human and animal wastes. These germs in water can lead to symptoms like diarrhea, headaches, nausea, and cramps.

- Keep hazardous chemicals, such as paint, fertilizer, pesticides, and motor oil, away from the well.

- Test water regularly.

- If any changes are noticed in the well or water, contact the county extension service or a licensed professional.

- Be cautious when mowing the grass near the well.

Do not damage the casing, which could jeopardize sanitary protection. Also, avoid piling snow, leaves, and other debris around or on top of the well.

If you do not have the history of your well or its age, check with the local town or city hall. They usually keep well records. In rural areas, neighbors are also a good source of information.

CASE STUDY: SEPTIC SYSTEM EXPERT

Dennis F. Hallahan
Professional Engineer
Technical Director at
Infiltrator Systems

The septic system is an important part of a home's plumbing system. "A septic system processes and purifies household and commercial waste (effluent). A standard septic system is typically installed on-site and has two components: a septic tank and a leach field or drain field," said Dennis F. Hallahan, PE. "The effluent consists of black water (toilet wastes) and gray water (kitchen sink, bathtub, and laundry wastes)." The septic tank provides treatment as helpful bacterial digests organic particles contained in the wastewater. Secondary treatment takes place once the water flows into the leach field. Bacteria complete the digestion and purification process as the wastewater slowly leaches into the soil.

Anyone who purchases an older home wonders if the septic systems work as well and as efficiently as other methods of waste removal. According to Hallahan, they are. "A properly installed and maintained septic system constructed from high-quality materials is a safe, efficient, and effective method of purifying wastewater. In a major 1997 report to Congress, the EPA stated that properly maintained on-site wastewater treatment systems (septic systems) were a fully viable, cost-effective alternative to sewer systems."

There are various septic systems available that incorporate tanks, filters, leach fields, and installation options. The local health department can help determine the best type of system needed based on a home's size, number of occupants, and the kinds of treatment features necessary for the home. They might suggest an infiltrator chamber. This is technically and environmentally a superior product for septic leach fields. They are made from recycled plastics, offer enhanced performance, have a long shelf life, and are easy to install.

Although many homeowners want to install their own septic systems this could end up being a costly mistake. The system's performance is based on the correct installation of both the septic tank and the leach field. Small mistakes or miscalculations can negatively influence the installation and the performance of the system. Experienced plumbers, who have experience working with septic systems, should do projects of this nature, unless the homeowner is fully versed and experienced in the area.

Deciding if a septic system needs to be repaired, remodeled, or replaced depends on a number of details, including local governmental codes, expected usage, and the specific home site. A professional plumber will be able to determine what needs to be done. The job of a septic system is simple, but the equipment can be complex. A well-designed, properly installed, and carefully maintained system is capable of decades of service, but like any other system, it will eventually need to be replaced. "There are a number of other causes for failure, but in a majority of cases, the system can be overloaded. When this occurs, water enters the system at a greater rate than it can be absorbed, causing a system back up," Hallahan said.

Hallahan said two of the most common questions among homeowners regarding septic systems are "Why do septic systems fail?" and "How do I know if mine is failing?" According to Hallahan, "if the liquid effluent cannot soak into the soil surrounding the leach field, sewage may back up into the system, creating two distinct symptoms: effluent surfacing on the ground at a location over the leach field or septic tank, or sewage backing up into the house. Symptoms of a failed septic system vary from surfacing effluent in the area of the disposal field, surfacing effluent over the septic tank, strong odors and green lush grass over the disposal field, or backed up plumbing and drains."

The most important question homeowners should ask is "How do I operate a healthy system?"

The following are Hallahan's suggestions for keeping the system running smoothly:

- Conserving water is a big step in keeping the system running smoothly. Untreated solids can be flushed out of the tank if large amounts of water go into the system during a short period of time. Use common-sense rules for conserving as much water as possible.

- Throughout the day, spread out heavy water-usage activities, such as washing clothes and showers.

- Collect rainwater and air conditioner water for use around house and for watering plants and gardens.

- Fix all dripping faucets.

- Replace old toilets that use up to 5 gallons per flush with high-efficiency toilets. Check local regulations because many areas order the installation of water-conserving fixtures.

- Turn off the faucet while brushing your teeth.

- When replacing appliances such as washing machines and dishwashers, buy high-efficiency models.

- Keep drains clean. If a waste product is not biodegradable, do not flush it or pour it down the drain.

- Do not flush cotton balls, cat litter, cotton swabs, diapers, cigarettes, or feminine-hygiene products down the toilet.

- Do not flush or dispose of paints, oils, chemical solvents, poisons, or pesticides down the drain.

- Do not allow cooking greases, oils, or fat to go down the drain.

- Use biologically safe disinfectants, antibacterial soaps, bathroom cleaners, and bleach whenever possible.

- Use landscaping to keep surface water under control.

- Deflect water from downspouts, roofs, driveways, and sump pumps.

- Encourage the growth of the proper plants and grasses over the septic system to avoid soil erosion. To soak up water, plant evergreens such as pines, spruce, and cypress near the leach field.

- Avoid planting water-loving trees.

- Do not drive over or park on the septic system to prevent damage.

- Do not dig in the leach field; do not put an outbuilding on top of it; and do not put concrete or blacktop over it.

Regular maintenance is crucial. Septic tanks should be pumped every three to five years — more often if there is a lot of water usage. Hire a professional for tank inspection, and keep a record of work done on the system.

CHAPTER 8

Interior Systems and Framework

Types of Heating Systems

The heating systems in older homes were not built with efficiency and today's energy costs in mind. As fuel costs have increased over the decades, so has the demand for energy-efficient systems. Consumers are motivated to replace their old and inefficient heating systems to save on heating and cooling bills.

Money saved is not the only concern. Today's consumers also want to protect the environment as well as use renewable energy products and resources. This chapter describes heating and cooling system options, maintenance and repair guidelines, what to look for when replacing an outdated system, and how to make a home more energy-efficient.

Forced hot air (FHA)

This is the most common type of heating systems in homes. Also known as a central air furnace, this heats the air and is distributed throughout the home via ductwork that enters the living space through floor or ceiling registers. Fans move the hot air through ducts, which are made out of metal, plastic, or fiberglass. Electricity, oil, natural gas, or propane gas can be used to fuel this system. Floor, wall, or ceiling ducts need to be periodically inspected for leaks so the system will function efficiently and properly.

The benefit of having ducts is they can carry air conditioning through the house, too. Ductwork can also be used for the ventilation, air filtration, dehumidification, humidification, and air purification of the house. FHA heats an area fast but is noisy. If considering this type of system, then realize that the installation of the ductwork can be expensive. Older homes are not necessarily conducive to concealing the ducts in a simple fashion. Some retrofitting might be required if space is suitable is limited to install ducts.

Advances in heating and air conditioning systems have benefited historic homeowners with limited space. The Unico System provides a resolution by implementing modular air handlers and coils into attics, ceilings, crawl spaces, and closets. These are pliable mini-ducts that can be directed through existing ceiling, floor and wall cavities. Installation of traditional, larger ductwork is no longer necessary.

This system circulates air throughout each room instead of just dumping air through ceiling or wall registers, which leads to drafts and hot/cold spots. The Unico System outlets are smaller and come in 5-inch round outlets or ½- by 8-inch slotted sidewall applications, so they fit nicely with any décor. Finally, if humidity is a problem in the home, the Unico System removes 30 percent more moisture from the air than conventional systems. To learn about this product, visit their Web site at **www.unicosystem.com**.

Electric baseboard heat

These are heaters that are affixed to the wall near floor level. They use electricity and have internal heating elements that heat the metal fins that eventually heat the room. Each heater can be zoned to have a thermostatic control, or it can have a central temperature control mechanism. Electric baseboard heaters are inexpensive to install but are not suitable as a single source of heat for cold climates because they are expensive to operate. They are best used in moderate climates or as an additional heating source in cold climates. Overall, electric baseboard heat is clean, quiet, inexpensive to install, and easy to zone — but expensive to operate.

Heat pumps

Heat pumps are an energy-efficient system that can both heat and cool the house through a mechanical device and electricity. They are better suited for moderate climates instead of climates with sub-freezing temperatures. They use ducts, but there are also ductless units available. The air-source heat pump is the most common type.

When the pump is heating, it evaporates the refrigerant located in an outdoor coil. The pump draws heat from the outside as liquid evaporates. Gas is compressed and moves into the inside coils. It condenses and releases the heat inside the house; when cooling, the opposite occurs.

The pump evaporates liquid from the heat inside the house's air. The gas, once compressed, moves to the outside coil and is condensed. This action releases the heat outside. There are pressure changes created by a compressor and expansion valve, which makes gas condense outside at a higher temperature and evaporate at indoors at this lower temperature.

Electric heat pumps

Electric heat pumps operate under the same principle as air conditioning systems. They use a compressor and electricity to compress a refrigerant from a gas to a liquid state. In cool weather, heat is generated and released inside to a warm house. In the hot weather, heat is released to the outside to cool the house. This type of system is inexpensive to run but expensive to install. It is important to have an annual maintenance checkup to keep the system running at its optimal level. Heat pumps lose their efficiency below 40 degrees, and this is where a geothermal heat pump is more suitable.

Geothermal heat pumps

Geothermal heat pumps operate similarly as the electric heat pumps, but instead use the natural heat from below the earth's surface to operate. Initially, they are expensive to install, but are lower in cost when it comes to the monthly utility bill. They can be used for both heating and cooling. A pump is installed above ground on a concrete pad, and then holes are drilled in the concrete to find energy pockets. Cool water is fed into the ground through pipes and is warmed by the geothermal energy in the ground. This warmer water is pumped back up to the surface and used to heat the home. Electricity is used to operate the pump, and the same system can cool the house.

Hot water boiler

In this system, the boiler heats water and pumps it through pipes to radiators that are dispersed throughout the house. Many older homes have radiators that are decorative. If damaged, these decorative radiators are difficult and costly to repair. In general, radiators create decorating dilemmas because furniture cannot be placed in front of them. Radiators need to be free of obstructions so they can properly disperse heat into the room. A boiler is easy to zone and quiet, but costly.

Hydronic heating — hot water baseboard

The hydronic heating system is also considered a radiant heating system. It uses a boiler to heat water. This water travels through tubes in baseboard units attached to walls. Overall, this system is quiet, can be easily zoned and controlled room by room, and is energy-efficient. The downside is, it takes longer to heat a room and cannot be used in conjunction with an air conditioning system. Also, furniture, curtains, or any other objects should not block the units.

Radiant heating

A radiant heating system can be installed in the floors, the ceilings, or the walls. The heat generated through a radiant heating system first warms the surface (floor, ceiling, or wall), then warms the room through the principle of infrared radiation (IR). This principle can be compared to the effect we feel from the heat coming from a fireplace when we are standing across the room from it. The following is a description of the three types of radiant heating systems: floor, ceiling, and walls:

Floor heat

Radiant floor heat is the most common type of radiant heating system. Once the floor is warm, the heat rises and warms the rest of the room or area. This system can easily be installed in older homes in a variety of ways that makes it an attractive option. Tile is the best floor covering for floor heating; it holds the heat and allows for more heat to radiate through the floors.

Thick carpeting and padding can prevent the heat from coming up efficiently. If using carpeting, it should be thin, and the padding should be dense. Wood floors can become dry from the heat, so it is best to use laminated-wood flooring.

There are three mediums that can generate floor heat: air, electricity, and water. Heat travels through tubing, which is made out of plastic (or metal for air) for water to travel through. When electricity is the energy source, electric elements are used to transfer the heat. Here is a description of each type:

- **Air** — This is only viable when used in conjunction with solar panels. The cost to heat air and force it through the tubing is not energy-efficient, and not a practical option for homes.

- **Electricity** — The cost of electricity can be prohibitive, so consider this option carefully. A thick slab of concrete above the electrical elements will allow the heat to warm the concrete during off-peak times and keep the home warm for many hours.

- **Water** — This is the most popular and energy-efficient method to transfer radiant floor heating. Water is heated in a boiler and pumped into the tubing. This method makes it easy to set up separate zones, and each room can have its own thermostat.

Floor heat tubing is installed in a variety of methods. Here are some common installation techniques:

- For new construction or for room addition, the tubing can be embedded in a concrete slab foundation. Although it takes time for concrete to heat, it holds heat for a long time and is a good medium to hold and distribute heat throughout the house.

- If a concrete slab already exists, tubing can be placed on top of it. Then, another thin layer of concrete can be poured, or another subfloor can be installed above the tubes.

- If the house has a crawl space or basement, the tubes can be installed under the subfloor. It will be necessary to drill through the floor joists and install a reflective insulating material underneath the tubing to reflect the heat upward.

- Tubes can be installed on framed floor decking, with a thin layer of concrete poured over the tubing.

Radiant wall heat

This system installs panels made of aluminum on the walls that are heated with electricity. Tubes carrying water can be used, but there is the potential of leakage and damage to the walls. The panels are expensive to install and operate; this system is viable as an alternative source of heat for a home or for a new room addition.

Ceiling panels

These are mounted on the surface and heat rooms through radiant heat transfer. They are made of dense fiberglass insulation boards mounted in a frame. They come with a heating element and often use electricity as its fuel source. They do not warm the air, but warm objects just like the sun does on a sunny day. They are conducive to zone heating, and each room can have its own thermostat. They use energy only in the rooms that require heat, which makes them more energy-efficient than other systems.

Radiant heat is efficient because heat is not lost through ducts. It is good for people with allergies because air is not blown throughout the house, where particles of dust or other allergens exist. These systems heat evenly and are easy to zone, but they are expensive to install.

Air Conditioning

Residential air conditioning was first offered in the late 1920s, but the Great Depression and World War II limited sales. Most homes built prior to 1945 will not have an air conditioning system. After 1945, many homeowners installed window air conditioning units or central air conditioning systems. The southern and western parts of the United States will usually have more central air systems, as compared to the northern and cooler climate states of New England.

> ### ASHRAE
>
> The American Society of Heating, Refrigerating, and Air Conditioning Engineers (ASHRAE) is a membership organization involved in conducting research, writing industry standards, publishing informative materials, and offering continuing education to those in the profession. To learn more about this society, visit their Web site at **www.ashrae.org**.

A central air conditioning system basically works like a refrigerator. The refrigerant (a gas) is compressed and becomes a liquid when it passes through coiled tubes in the evaporator. The air in the home passes over these coils and, when pressure is released, the gas absorbs the heat from the air. This cooler air travels through the ductwork and comes out of registers placed throughout the house. The gas (heat) is pumped to the condenser located outside and recompressed, and the heat is discharged outside.

Homes with forced hot-air systems are perfect for a central air system because they already have the ductwork installed. The expensive part of installing a central air conditioning system is finding a way to install the ducts in an older home. They can be installed in ceilings, walls, floors, closets, attics, and basements. Installers need to get creative to find the best and least disruptive path.

Installation is ideal when a house is being gutted and there are more open spaces to use. Electrical service needs to be 200 amps for central air. If cost is prohibitive, consider installing individual window or wall units. Some do not like to use window or wall units in an older or historic home because it detracts from the appearance.

Another alternative is individual room air conditioners. These are floor models and can be rolled from room to room. The excess condensation needs to be vented out a window but will be less obtrusive in appearance than a window or wall unit.

> ### Size matters
>
> A central air unit needs to be the proper size for a house. If it is too big it could lead to too much humidity in the house. This happens because when air meets the cooling coils the air condenses, water develops and is drained away. This makes the air in the house cool and dry. If the unit is too large for the house, the unit will shut off before the air has a chance to be sufficiently dehumidified. This can cause the moist air to remain in the house and eventually develop into mold and mildew on surfaces and inside walls.

Making the air in a home healthy

Dust, allergens, pet dander, mites, mold, smoke, spores, and other pollutants can make the air inside a home unhealthy and cause problems, for those with allergies. The key is to properly ventilate the home so that there is enough fresh air circulating throughout. This is done by enhancing and improving the current heating and cooling systems. There are two methods: air cleaners and heat recovery ventilators that lessen the pollutants in a home. The following is information on both options:

Air cleaners

Here are the options to consider if a house has stale or unhealthy air, or if inhabitants have allergies and breathing problems:

1. Small tabletop or room air filtration units clean the air in a designated area.

2. Central air cleaners can be installed in conjunction with a central air conditioning system's ductwork.

3. Furnace filters can be used in conjunction with central heat and air systems. There are different levels of filtration available for purchase. Effectiveness and features are directly related to retail price. The following are filters listed according to price:

    a. Spun-glass filters are the least expensive option but are not very effective. They only remove about 10 percent of the large particulates in the air and have limited success in capturing the smaller particles. They need to be changed on a monthly basis. They do not remove smaller particulates in the air because the weave in the fiberglass is too large.

    b. Pleated filters have a larger surface area, so they catch more particulates as the air passes over the pleats. Although more expensive than the fiberglass filters, they do a better job and typically last for two to four months.

HVAC — What does it mean?

HVAC is a familiar abbreviation many consumers see on the side of contractor vans. It stands for heating, ventilation, and air-conditioning (HVAC). When in need of a new heating system, contact an HVAC contractor to calculate what size of heating/cooling system is best for the house. Make sure to evaluate a system that has earned the ENERGY STAR rating. This equipment helps consumers save on their heating bills.

c. A true high-efficiency particulate air (HEPA) filter is not usually used in home heating systems. They are too dense and would restrict the airflow for a residential furnace. Pleated HEPA filters are similar to the ones mentioned above, but they are made of a denser material, so they catch more of the smaller particulates.

d. Electrostatic filters use the principle of static electricity to remove particles from the air, just like when clothing sticks to the body with static electricity. They are the most expensive option in furnace filters but do the best job. They are reusable and washable, and are a more effective option as long as they are washed according to the manufacturer's directions. They trap more dust and pollutants, and are a good investment — especially for those with allergies.

Heat-recovery ventilators

A home that is airtight is good for saving on heating and cooling bills, but is bad when it comes to breathing in fresh air. Older homes are notorious for being drafty and not being insulated. To save on energy costs, homeowners try to make their older homes more efficient, insulated, and draft-free, but the air quality in the house suffers.

A heat-recovery ventilator (HRV) is a system that uses blowers and ducts to move fresh air in and stale air out. One duct removes stale and moist air through an HRV unit and blows it outside. The second duct brings the fresh air. Both types of air separately pass through a heat exchanger core, which captures energy from the stale air so there is a minimal amount of heated or cooled air lost to the outside.

This core does not capture 100 percent of the energy, so some of it is lost. When a home has forced hot air heat, the HRV is attached to this system. If there is another type of heating system, the HRV is connected to outdoor air ducts.

Tips to improve a home's quality of air

- Install vents in kitchens and bathrooms to remove cooking odors and moisture.
- Vent wood stoves and fireplaces properly.
- Open windows when weather permits.
- Directly vent clothes dryers and central vacuum cleaning systems to the outdoors.
- Make sure to store paints, cleaners, pesticides, and other toxic solvents away from where residents live in the house.
- Minimize or do not smoke in the home.
- Never barbecue in the home.
- Keep pets outdoors or limit their time indoors; keep them brushed and clean.

Maintenance and Minor Repairs

Conducting regular maintenance and fixing minor repairs on the heating and cooling systems are just as important as changing the oil in and tuning up an automobile. It is best to resolve any problems before the heating and cooling seasons are under way. The following are tips on how to properly maintain the systems to prevent emergency service calls and costly repairs:

Heating and cooling systems: Maintenance tips

- All systems should be kept clean. Dust, debris, and buildup will cause a system to run less efficiently.
- For all types of heating and cooling systems, have a professional conduct a pre-season checkup: one for the heating system in the fall, and one for the cooling system in late spring.

A typical checkup will include the following:

- Ensure that all electrical connections are tight.

- Measure the electrical voltage and current on any motors.
- Lubricate all moving parts.
- Check thermostat settings.
- Check system controls.
- Check that the condensation drain is not plugged.
- Check the conditioner's refrigerant level.
- Clean air conditioning coils and blower.
- Check gas and oil connections, the gas pressure, and the heat exchanger.

Hot-air systems

- Replace the air filters in a hot-air system as recommended by the manufacturer.
- Inspect ductwork for leaks or tears; repair these.

Hot-water systems

- **Water evaporates in heating systems while they are in operation in the winter** — Add water to the system in the fall prior to putting on the heat. This will replace the water lost during the previous season.

- **During the winter, sediment will form and lie at the bottom of the boiler** — This needs to be eliminated by draining the boiler. Boilers have a water faucet. Before turning the heat on for the season, open the water valve and let clean water run through the boiler to flush it out. Run the water until it is clear, then refill the boiler with clean water.

- **Radiators need to be bled before turning on the heat** — Air collects in radiators in the spring and summer, and must be eliminated before the fall and winter heating season. Start with the radiators on the top floor and work down to the bottom floor.

Find the small valve near the top of each radiator and open this valve. Hold a small bucket under the valve. Opening the valve lets the air out. As soon as water starts to come out, close the valve. Do this same process during the middle of the heating season, too.

Make sure radiators are working properly by checking the following:

- **Check for leaks** — If the leaks appear to come from the radiator, then it must be repaired. If the leak comes from a cap nut, tighten it with one wrench while holding the valve still with another wrench.

- **Make sure valves are open all the way or closed all the way, not just halfway.**

- **Check all the radiators in the house and make sure they have a slope slightly toward the pipe that leads out from the floor** — This helps to alleviate noises coming from the furnace. If the radiator is level with the floor, then use a ¼-inch wooden wedge to lift it up slightly.

- **Make sure all vents are clean and clear** — These release the air from inside the radiator and, if blocked, the radiator will not properly operate. Vents are available at the local hardware store and are easy to replace. Clean and clear vents will ensure that the radiator heats the room properly.

Replacing a heating system

Replacing a heating system can be a costly expense. Installing a new system usually involves the expertise of both electrical and plumbing contractors, and the system needs to be installed according to local and state building codes. Make sure contractors apply for the proper permits and inspections to prevent delays. Many communities require licensed professionals to install a heating system, so unless homeowners have licenses, they will be required to hire a professional for this job.

Local utility companies can provide guidance and suggestions on a suitable system to purchase. Many will install them for the homeowner; however, the cost is typically higher than hiring a commercial contractor. On the other hand, many utility companies offer attractive financing options. Find out if the utility company has any rebates for installing a new and energy-efficient system. Also, determine if there are any discounts on fuel rates with the installation of a new system.

The house and its surroundings determine the efficiency of the heating and air system. Here are factors that make a difference:

- Location of a house in regard to southern or northern exposure.

- The trees around the house providing shade and breaking the impact of wind.

- If the house has no cracks and openings, it will be more energy-efficient.

- The amount of insulation or lack of insulation will have an impact on efficiency.

- The humidity levels, in different regions around the country, is a factor to consider when controlling moisture in a house and the implications it has for the heating and cooling systems.

Usually it is best to replace a system with the same type of heat delivery system that is currently in place. This is usually the least expensive option, although it is still worth the effort to research other options before making the final choice. A qualified heating contractor or engineer can evaluate the home for viable alternatives.

Rules to live by when replacing a heating system

When replacing a heating system, remember the following tips:

- Buy a system that local heating contractors can repair when there is a problem.

- Local utility companies can offer suggestions as to heating systems that are popular and efficient in your area.

- After installation, faithfully follow the manufacturer's recommended maintenance schedule. Contact the manufacturer if you lose the owner's manual. They may have extras or offer the owner's manual in an electronic format.

- Do not skimp on quality — buy a good-quality system.

- A simple system is a less expensive system.

- Less is more; do not buy too big of a heating system. Too much heating capacity makes a system turn on and off frequently, which leads to parts wearing out and the system working less efficiently.

- When replacing a system, talk to a heating engineer or Heating, Ventilation, and Air Conditioning (HVAC) contractor who can offer advice on the best system for your house based on its size and design.

Make sure local building codes are adhered to when the new system is installed. Typically, a plumber and electrician are required for installation. A roofing contractor might need to do work where pipes, ducts, and ventilators pass through the ceiling or roof. Most homeowners turn to a professional to install a new system, but for those who are proficient at electrical and plumbing work — and who can meet codes and pass inspections — they might choose to install their own system.

How to save on the heating bill

There are many simple yet-inexpensive ways to save on a heating bill. Modifications in one's behavior and low-cost repairs around a house will pay off. To find out if a home has a good energy-efficiency score, take the "Do-It-Yourself Home Energy Audit" found on the U.S. Department of Energy's Web site at **www.energysavers.gov/your_home/energy_audits/ index.cfm/mytopic=11170**.

Changing habits to save

Here are behavior changes that will make a difference in heating bills:

- Put on a sweater when you feel cold instead of turning up the thermostat. According to the U.S. Department of Energy, consumers can save up to 1 percent on their heating bills for every degree they lower their thermostat.

- Keep trees and shrubs pruned around the house that might block sunlight.

- Kitchen and bathroom exhaust fans draw heat out of the house, so limit their use.

- Close the damper when a fireplace or woodstove is not in use. Heat is drawn up the chimney. Glass doors on a fireplace can help to keep heat from being sucked up the chimney, as long as they are kept closed.

- Do not use a stove (or oven) to heat the kitchen because it is dangerous and a waste of energy.

- Make sure to dust radiators and the heat vents. Dust will act as insulator and slow the heating system from working properly.

- Schedule an annual heating system checkup before using the system.

Do-it-yourself projects

The following are some simple projects homeowners can do to save on the heating bill:

- Use caulk to fill cracks and holes where air is coming into the house. This tends to happen around the windows and doors. Select the right caulk for the project.

- Put weather stripping around the doors and windows to block air from coming into the house and heat going out.

- Put duct tape around heating ducts where the heat is leaking out.

- Use insulation to wrap around pipes to prevent them from freezing and to save on energy. Do not forget to insulate the water heater.

- Replace the old and dried-out putty around windows.

Long-term investments and improvements

- Consider installing a wood-burning stove or fireplace.
- Use insulated drapes and curtains to block heat and cold drafts.
- Get a programmable thermostat with an automatic timer.

When not home, lower the temperature and program the thermostat to raise the temperature prior to returning home.

- Heat by zones, and only heat rooms that are currently in use.
- Insulate the floors over unheated spaces such as garages, basements, and crawl spaces.
- Replace old appliances and heating systems with ENERGY STAR-labeled products. Do not forget to check the efficiency ratings before making the purchase.

Final suggestions

- Learn about Federal tax credits for the replacement of energy efficient upgrades on appliances, windows, and hot water heaters at the ENERGY STAR Web site, **www.energystar.gov,** and click the "Tax Credits for Energy Efficiency" tab.

- Ask the local utility company for ideas on how to save on heating costs. Some offer a free home energy audit and will make suggestions on how to save.

- Find out if your state has incentive programs for renewable energy and energy-efficiency through the U.S. Department of Energy's Database of State Incentives for Renewable & Efficiency's Web site: at **www.dsireusa.org**.

- Senior citizens, low-income citizens, and unemployed consumers might find assistance from their state, utility providers, or government assistance program. Many utilities have different payment plans for senior citizens on a fixed income.

- The U.S. Department of Energy (DOE) has the Weatherization Assistance Program that helps low-income families make beneficial long-term changes to lower their energy bills. To learn more, visit their Web site at **http://apps1.eere.energy.gov/ weatherization**.

Solving Moisture Problems

Excess moisture in the home creates problems such as mold, mildew, decay, and deterioration. The degree of moisture depends upon the style of house, the foundation and how airtight it is, insulation level, climate, and location of the house on the lot. Much of the excess moisture is caused from leaks in roofs and pipes, poor drainage around the house, and driving rain.

Although it is thought that the basement is the area in a house that has the most problems with moisture, this is not always the case. Moisture can be found in all levels of a house. Solving moisture problems begins with an investigation and analysis of the situation. Telltale signs of excess moisture in the home are the following:

- Mold
- Mildew
- Musty odors
- Condensation
- Stains or discolorations on walls
- Wet or damp wood
- Blistering or peeling of exterior paint
- Efflorescence (a white powdery substance on brick, concrete or stone)

Solutions

Once it is determined there is a moisture problem, take corrective action to prevent further damage. There are both simple and inexpensive solutions, and costly and complicated solutions available. The following are solutions to problems that are common in older homes.

1. Use dehumidifiers in areas of the house where there is excess moisture. They have square-foot capacity levels, so be sure to get one that can handle the space. Dehumidifiers are used during the summer months when there is more moisture in the air. They have a container that fills with the excess water. Run the dehumidifier only when water is being generated. Do not run excessively because the motor will run out sooner. A general rule of thumb is to run the machine continually when at least 1 gallon of water is being collected in a 24-hour period. If less water is being collected, then run for a few hours a day.

2. Install exhaust fans in the kitchen, laundry room, and bathrooms. Vent them to the outside instead of letting the exhaust go to the attic or other parts of the house.

3. Repair all roof and plumbing leaks immediately so they do not turn into moisture problems later.

4. Make sure gutters and downspouts are installed properly and move water away from the house. Make sure gutters are large enough to handle the volume of water generated for the rainfall in your area. Make sure there are enough downspouts to move the water properly.

5. Clean gutters in the spring and the fall (after leaves have completely fallen).

6. Make sure the soil and landscaping around the house is properly graded and at a slope so water is diverted away from the house.

7. Use a sump pump to move excess water away from and out of the house during steady periods of rain. Sump pumps are typically located in a pit in the basement and have a hose or tubing that carries the water to the outside and away from the house. Some pumps will automatically turn on when they sense a certain level of water is present; others have to be manually turned on. Many a basement has flooded because no one was home to turn on the pump. Installing an automatic system prevents this from happening.

8. Vapor-diffusion retarders (VDRs) are used to reduce the amount of water vapor in a house. They come in a membrane form or as a coating. Membranes come in thick and thin versions. Thick VDRs include rigid-foam insulation panels, aluminum, stainless steel, and reinforced plastic. These are fastened to walls and sealed at their seams. The thinner membranes come in rolls of aluminum and paper-faced fiberglass insulation, for foil-backed wallboard and a polyethylene plastic sheet. Coatings in the form

of paint also work to effectively minimize water vapor, especially in warmer climates.

9. If these precautionary steps do not resolve the problem, contact a professional moisture control specialist to further evaluate the situation and offer a solution.

Electrical and Plumbing

The electrical and plumbing systems are the veins and energy source for the whole house. Those who live in older homes should consider upgrading these systems for their own comfort, safety, and efficiency. The upgrades and improvements can be costly, but they offer a great deal of comfort and peace in the home. The building codes of many communities require permits for electrical and plumbing upgrades and repairs; therefore, it will be necessary to hire professionals to complete these projects. Check with local codes before proceeding to fix or repair electrical and plumbing systems.

Safety Always Comes First

Safety is always a concern with any home renovation project, but this is even more critical when it comes to working with electricity. The electrical systems in older homes may have corroded with age and can be a fire hazard. In addition, they might not be adequate for today's appliances and electronic equipment. These are the two main reasons homeowners change or upgrade their electrical systems. A homeowner can decide the best course of action by having a basic understanding of the home's current system.

Before beginning any electrical work, check with the local city or town for specifications and requirements. If permits and inspections are required, then follow the local and state building codes. Some communities will not allow a homeowner (or anyone else) to perform their own electrical work unless they have a current electrician's license.

For do-it-yourselfers, it is best to contact a licensed electrician for a professional opinion and estimate on the cost to bring the house up to code. If the cost is prohibitive, then make changes in phases. Take care of any safety hazards first.

Electricity Basics

A three-bedroom house should have at least 100 amps of service. If considering installing central air conditioning, then upgrade to 200 amps of service. Some of today's kitchen appliances require 200 amps. New circuits may need to be added to accommodate the many small and large kitchen appliances used today. Older homes were not wired to simultaneously accommodate the use of blenders, microwave ovens, coffeemakers, and dishwashers. A trend in bathroom renovations is to create a spa, but those extra amenities might require additional outlets and circuits.

Upgrading electrical service

The rooms in a house that require the most electrical outlets and power are the kitchen, the bathroom, the basement (if there is one), and the laundry room. Many older homes have inadequate power to these high-need rooms. When electrical service is upgraded, the electrical capacity is potentially increased in the home by adding more outlets and circuits.

This electrical service upgrade does not mean there is an increase in the number of circuits or outlets, or power to the rooms in the house. The upgrade creates the possibility to increase the number of outlets in a home. In order for capacity to change, new circuits need to be added — this usually means additional wires need to be run to the kitchen (and other rooms) from the new service panel. These costs are still a necessary and worthwhile investment.

The only factors that change with an upgrade in electrical service are the following:

- The physical connections between the home and the electrical power distribution grid. A power plant continues to supply the electricity to the grid.

- An electric meter and the cables connected to the meter. Meters are usually the property of the local utility company, and they will come out to install the new meter. The meter measures how much electricity the people in the house uses. Customers are charged for their electrical service based on the amount of kilowatt hours that are used (1 kilowatt hour = 1,000 watts per hour). For example, if you turn on 10 lamps with 100-watt light bulbs each, then for one hour you will be charged for one kilowatt of power. Utility companies put a security tag on the electric meter so individuals cannot tamper with the meter.

- Electrical distribution panel is changed. This is the main service panel that carries the electrical power from the grid to all the outlets and receptacles in the house.

- A grounding system is put in place to prevent electrical shock to inhabitants of the house.

The electrical service is connected to the ground through the means of a copper wire. The copper wire is inside a metal conduit, which is attached to an underground water pipe.

If you do not have enough outlets or electrical power in your kitchen, this upgrade will not improve this condition. A new distribution panel, wiring, and circuits, however, can be fed to the kitchen to accommodate a family's daily activities. The other benefit to these upgrades is safety. It is not always possible to see safety hazards in the home, but upgrading electrical service is a good way to create a safe environment.

The National Electric Code

The National Fire Protection Agency wrote the National Electric Code — a set of standards for the professionals installing electrical wiring and electrical products. The agency compiles a handbook every three years with updates. The main focus is safety and fire prevention.

Replacing the old fuse box

Fuse boxes, although considered old-fashioned, are still being manufactured and are a viable option for electrical service. Some electrical contractors will advise switching to a modern circuit panel, but the most important consideration in making this decision is to make sure the system is adequate and safe for the home.

Wiring found in older homes

There are a few different types of old wiring found in older homes. The following is a summary of them:

- **Knob-and-tube wiring** — This is from the 1890s through 1920s (and some homes even had it until the 1940s). It has rubber-coated conductors strung on porcelain insulators.

- **ATTIX cable** — This is from the early 1900s through 1920s and has a rubber insulation of individual conductors. In the late 1940s, the rubber insulation became obsolete when vinyl chloride plastic was invented.

- **Bx galvanized steel cable (armored cable)** — This was used from 1930 to 1960s and is a General Electric brand.

Electrical terminology

Service equipment — The circuit breakers, switches, and fuses that connect the load end of service conductors coming into the house.

Watts — Power consumption or the amount of electricity used.

GFCI — Ground-fault circuit interrupter; a circuit breaker installed to protect people from electrical shock by shutting off power to an outlet if the device senses an imbalance in an electrical circuit.

Ground — When a connection ensues between the electrical circuit (or equipment) and earth, or to a conducting entity acting in place of the earth, either intentionally or by accident.

Volts — This is the unit of electrical pressure.

Ohms — This is the measure of electrical resistance.

Amperage (amps) — The rate and strength of the electrical current is measured in amps, so amperage equal watts/volts.

Circuit breaker — The circuit breaker is the device that opens and closes the electrical circuit by use of a toggle switch.

Conduit — This is a tube-shaped pathway for electrical wires. It is made out of metal or heavy-duty plastic.

If the electrical system in an older home is safe and adequate, leave it alone. If it is not, however, assess what needs to be fixed or upgraded, and make a plan to complete the work. If the electrical service is not adequate for daily living, then add electrical circuits instead of new service. If completely gutting the interior of the house, get new service and wiring if more power is needed, and if the old wiring is unsafe. Consider doing some of the work yourself. If the whole system needs to be re-wired or a new circuit breaker needs to be installed, do not attempt these types of projects unless you have the experience to do the work and are confident in your abilities.

Electrical don'ts

- Do not work with electricity unless you understand how it works.

- Do not work in a service panel or remove the cover. Leave this to the electrician. Even though a main fuse or breaker is shut off, there are still wires that are live.

- Do not tamper with the electric meter. This is the property of the utility company. Call them if you need help.

- Do not work without the proper electrical tools. They are specifically made to complete the work safely.

Underwriters laboratories

Electrical materials need to be new and listed with Underwriters Laboratories® (UL). This is an independent, global organization involved in promoting product safety and certification. They have been around for more than 100 years and still continue to test products and write safety standards. Their seal of approval can be found on electrical materials they are certified as safe. To learn more about their organization, visit their Web site at **www.ul.com/global/eng/pages**.

Smoke Detectors

Smoke detectors (alarms) are safety devices that warn of a potentially hazardous fire developing in a home. A loud signal alarm will go off to inform residents to vacate the premises and seek emergency assistance. Smoke alarms save lives. They first came into existence in the 1970s, and today these valuable devices can be purchased for under $10 — making it possible to have one in every bedroom.

If the home is multi-level, be sure to place smoke detectors on each level. It is not necessary to place smoke alarms in kitchens, garages, attics, or crawl spaces. In addition to installing smoke detectors, each family should have an evacuation plan in place and practice it on a regular basis, especially with children. There are two types of smoke detectors:

- **Ion detectors** — Reacts to open flames quicker; it is the least expensive.

- **Photoelectric** — Reacts quicker to smoldering flames; does not react as quickly to cooking heat/smoke.

Installing detectors

Many building codes across the nation require smoke detectors in the home. They can be battery-operated or wired into the home's electrical system. When they are attached to the electrical system, they can all be interconnected so when one alarm goes off, they all go off. There is a power light that will indicate it is working. Some alarms will have an auxiliary 9-volt battery inside as a backup in case the electricity goes off. This alleviates the risk of not being alerted to potential danger because of a dead battery.

For safety's sake, do not disconnect the battery when it makes a chirping noise. This noise is a warning signal that the battery needs to be changed. A good rule of thumb is to replace the battery every January 1. To install an alarm, adhere to the following guidelines:

- Install alarms on the ceiling or high up on a wall.

- The top of an alarm should not be installed closer than 4 inches from a ceiling; do not install an alarm more than 12 inches from a ceiling.

- Install alarms at least 3 feet from the supply registers of a forced hot-air heating system.

- Do not install any closer than a distance of 3 feet from a kitchen door.

- Do not install smoke detectors any closer than a distance of 3 feet from a bathroom that contains a shower.

- Do not place a detector on a ceiling or an exterior wall below any unheated attic, if it is poorly insulated. This difference in temperature could prevent the smoke from reaching the alarm and will not alert occupants. Instead, place the detector on inside walls.

- If the home is occupied by senior citizens or disabled adults, place detectors on the wall instead of on the ceiling. Put them 12 inches down from the ceiling so it will be easier to change the batteries.

Make sure to follow the manufacturer's suggestions on testing the smoke detectors. A good rule of thumb is to test them once a month. To learn more about smoke detectors and smoke alarms, visit the Consumer Product Safety Commission's Web site at **www.cpsc.gov/cpscpub/pubs/ pub_idx.html**.

CHAPTER 9

Windows, Flooring, and Walls

Windows and Skylights

Although windows and skylights can theoretically be considered structural elements of a house, they are still opportunities to express a creative design style. Many older homes will have their original windows and doors, and these may need to be repaired, restored, or replaced. Skylights, on the other hand, are a newer feature for homes.

The history of glass and windows is very interesting. In studying the homes of the early settlers in the United States, we find that there were very few windows installed. The cost to manufacture glass and install a window was high, so only the wealthy could afford them. Glass, although expensive and a risk to ship, was sent to the colonies from England.

It was not until the mid 1700s that glass-manufacturing plants were established in the United States. There is a slight disagreement over where the first plant was located — either in Boston, Massachusetts, or Brooklyn, New York. Throughout the 1800s, there was speedy improvement with glass technology, and by the 1860s, plate glass lit up stores and office buildings in Europe and North America. Leading world manufacturers of the product include France, Belgium, and Germany. In 1883, European plate glass imports declined, and the Pittsburgh Plate Glass Co. became the first triumphant manufacturer in the United States.

The number of windows in a home still signifies wealth and quality of construction. One of the most expensive projects to tackle in a home is the replacement of old windows for newer, better-quality, energy-efficient windows.

What is glass?

Glass is a combination of coarse sand, soda ash, and other materials transformed into smooth transparent forms. On average, a batch mix used to manufacture flat glass materials comprises about 70 percent silica sand, 13 percent lime, 12 percent soda, and small amounts of other components. Today, recycled glass makes up about one-quarter of this batch. This glass has gone through cleaning and crushing, and has survived operations from previous glassmaking.

Today's technology has created many options in windows. Replacing windows is a costly project but adds value to a home and helps to save on energy costs. The age of the home and the condition of the windows determines whether they should be repaired or replaced.

Here are questions to evaluate the condition of your windows:

- Do they operate?
- Are they loose-fitting, or are they a poor fit for the frame?
- Are they energy-efficient?
- Do they lose heat or air conditioning?
- Are the sashes or sills rotted or decayed?
- Is the glazing putty or caulk loose, missing, or in need of replacement?

- Are they painted shut?
- Does the latch work and offer any security?
- Do you have storm and/or screen windows, and are they functioning properly?
- Are there windows with broken glass that need to be replaced?

Repairing windows is a great do-it-yourself project, if you have some time, skill, and patience. Making minor repairs saves on the cost of replacing windows.

Common repairs

Glazing windows involves removing old putty and replacing it with new. If the putty in your windows is deteriorating, it is time to replace it. Glazing might also have to be done if a pane is broken. It is easy to break the glass when trying to remove the old putty. Here are a few tips:

1. Use these tools: glazing compound putty; chisel and hammer; putty knife; glazing points; glass cleaner; and rags.

2. Clean away old putty. If the putty was from before the year 1978, you should be concerned about lead paint. To soften the putty, do not use a heat gun because this could cause a fire, break the glass, and release lead paint fumes into the air. Using a chisel, angle it in such a way that it will not hit the glass.

   If you are glazing several windows and painting your wooden house, try a product called The Silent Paint Remover™, which costs between $400 and $500. It uses infrared heat that will not get hot enough to release lead from your paint. Read more about it from the manufacturer's Web site at **www.silentpaintremover. com**. There is also a good article about the subject of paint removal on This Old House's Web site at **www.thisoldhouse.com/toh/ article/0,,386353,00.html**.

3. Clean sash and glass (if it is still in one piece) well.

4. Replace glass if this was part of the repair.

5. If glass is loose, push in some glazing points to keep the glass in place. Try not to push the pins into the glass — angle them in such a way as to not break the glass.

6. It is best to use a new can of glazing compound, or one that is fresh and moist. Put a gob down and spread out at a 45-degree angle with a putty knife. Glazing compound is very forgiving, and you will learn the technique with a little practice. It takes between three and five days to dry. Check the can for details. If working outside, it is best to not do if it will rain. The instructions will also give temperature guidelines.

Window replacement tips

If the home's windows are old, creaky, and energy-inefficient, then making the decision on whether to replace the old windows becomes more complex than one might think. There are different options that might offer a solution other than just replacing the windows, and there are different types of windows to choose. Consider the following scenarios when deciding:

-   If the original windows are still in the house but in a state of disrepair, is it better to repair them back to their original functional ability, or replace them with the same type of window or some other type of window? If the house is historic, then it is important to maintain the architectural integrity of the windows, so fixing them is the best option. If the house is older, then decide if replacing them with something similar or a different style makes sense.

- Did a previous owner replace the original windows with cheap or inefficient replacements? If this is the case, then consider replacing them with windows that are like the home's original windows. If it is decided to replace the old windows with ones that match the original style of the house, and you do not know what the originals looked like, then take a walk around your neighborhood. It is likely there are houses with a similar style to yours to match.

- What is more important — character or efficiency? Many think that their old and drafty windows are useless and inefficient. This might be true. However, with repairs and storm windows, they might be just as or more efficient as new double-glazed windows.

- What conveniences do new windows offer? They can be a breeze to clean and easier to open and close.

- What material should I choose for my windows? Wood is a good choice, but the material does eventually decay, so it need to be painted and sealed periodically.

- If the exterior of the windows is made out of vinyl, then the windows will eventually need refurbishing and cannot be painted or taken apart to repair; they will have to be replaced. Because of the way they are installed, if they need to be replaced, any siding or any other exterior shingles around the window casing will need to be replaced, too.

- There are aluminum-clad windows that can be installed, but one of the problems with them is that water can seep under the installation flange and rot the wood below. Fiberglass is another material now being used to manufacture windows. They are very stable, energy-efficient, paintable, and do not decay.

New windows are costly; therefore, if the budget is limited, consider replacing them in two phases. Replace the most important ones first, which are the front and side street windows. The second phase of the project will be to replace the remaining windows, but do this in six to 12 months. Do not wait too long to begin on the second phrase.

This is important for a few reasons. First, you want the windows to age uniformly so that if they are replaced within a year, the first batch of new windows will not look older than the second batch. Second, it increases the chances of being able to get the same style and model from a manufacturer. Choosing a standard style of window helps to ensure being able to match all the windows in the house.

The costs of replacing windows can be costly, so know what you are getting prior to purchasing. Cost varies and depends on the following factors:

- Does the house have standard-sized windows?

- What level of quality do you want? There are different quality levels in windows. A wood-framed window might cost more, but it might fit the character of the house better. Will a vinyl replacement window look out of place with the design or historic nature of the house?

- Will you install just a new sash in the current frame, or will you install both a new frame and sash?

- How many windows need to be purchased?

- Will you hire someone to do the installation, or will you do it yourself?

- Does repair work need to be done on the window frames prior to installing the new windows?

It is important to choose new windows wisely and not jump at the lowest priced ones available. The first step is to take measurements of all the windows. Second, decide if you plan to install them yourself or if professional installation will be required. Third, it is important to get at least three quotes from reputable sources and compare exactly what you will be getting for the price. Try to get a contract from anyone replacing the windows. Large home improvement retailers offer name brands and installation, but smaller window specialty businesses should also be included in the mix of quotes prior to making a decision.

CASE STUDY: AN ALTERNATIVE WINDOW FOR ENERGY EFFICIENCY

David Degling
Innerglass Window Systems, LLC
15 Herman Drive
Simsbury, CT 06070
800-743-6207
www.stormwindows.com

Just as eyes are the windows of the souls, the windows provide one of a historic house's distinctive characteristics. When the windows in an older home are in need of improvement, consider repairing instead of replacing them. If, after a thorough inspection, it is determined they are not able to be repaired, then find a suitable replacement that has the most similar characteristics of the original windows. However, if the existing windows are repairable but are energy-inefficient, historic preservationists encourage homeowners to repair these older gems and install storm windows, instead of installing new, contemporary-style windows.

Storm windows are a viable option, but one of the difficulties is finding mass-produced storm windows that fit the different sizes of windows found in older homes and that look attractive. Many older and historic homes might already have exterior storm windows installed, but they might also take away from the beauty and charm of the old windows. Instead of opting to replace these older windows with new windows or exterior storm windows, consider installing interior storm windows.

Innerglass Window Systems, LLC has created an alternative to installing outside storm windows and new windows. "The Innerglass product is not a replacement window, nor is it a storm window," said owner David Degling. "It takes the best features of each and creates a custom interior window made to fit the unique shape and sizes of older and historic homes. They are custom-designed to mount on the inside of the window and cannot been seen from the outside. They are made of a vinyl-framed glass window with a compression-fit mechanism."

One of the frustrations homeowners face in finding storm windows is getting them to fit. The Innerglass windows seal tightly, and there are no unsightly tracks because they mount with a concealed, stainless-steel springing system. They can easily be put in the window in the winter months and removed in the spring so windows to let in fresh air.

"We have a unique mounting system, which smoothly accommodates windows that are not square or are crooked," Degling said. "The spring-loaded design automatically compensates for out-of-square conditions, and the end result eliminates drafts, condensation, and lessens outside noises while allowing the homeowner to enjoy their beautiful old windows. Of course, we need exact measurements to make the windows. They are delivered to the home and do not need professional installation, but are made for do-it-yourselfers."

To learn more about these windows, figure out how to take exact measurements, and view a list of the historic properties Innerglass has made windows for, visit their Web site at **www.stormwindows.com**. If you are thinking about ways to repair and make a home's windows more energy-efficient, there is a useful article to read on the National Park Service Web site. The title of the article is "Weatherization and Improving the Energy Efficiency of Historic Buildings" and can be found at **www.nps. gov/history/hps/tps/weather/index.html**.

Skylights

Skylights have improved greatly over the last 25 years and are a welcome addition to a home to bring in more light and circulation. Skylights let in more light per unit area than regular windows; they project light more evenly over a space. Skylights are an inexpensive way to transform a room so it feels more spacious and bright. They offer some heat in winter months when it is sunny, and in the summer they can be propped open for ventilation to improve circulation and remove some of the heat in the room that naturally rises.

Leaking problems may be encountered when skylights are improperly installed or constructed. With single-paned skylights, issues with condensation may occur. For added energy-efficiency, use skylights with at least two glass panes and a heat-reflecting coating.

Skylights may be made of plastic or glass, and they can be fixed or operable. They are made in a variety of sizes, shapes, and styles.

Repairing a skylight is similar to repairing a leak in the roof:

1. For a shingle roof, gently lift up on the shingles around and near the skylight (use caution; do not break the shingles). Brush out any dirt, leaves, or debris.

2. Armed with a caulk gun with either a urethane roofing cement or silicone caulk, squeeze the cement under the shingles and into the area where shingles meet the skylight flange and the roofing felt.

3. Caulk any seams or joints to fix any leaks.

Floor Plans

There are three typical functional areas designated in a floor plan of a house. They are:

1. **Working**
    a. Kitchen
    b. Laundry
    c. Office
    d. Workshop
    e. Storage
    f. Garage

2. **Recreation**
    a. Living room
    b. Dining room
    c. Great room
    d. Family room
    e. Den
    f. Recreation room
    g. Finished basement

3. **Privacy**
    a. Bedrooms
    b. Bathrooms

When thinking about the floor plan and whether it needs changing, it is important to consider the following questions:

- How do people walk through the house?
- Where are the interior and exterior door openings?
- Are there enough windows in the house to offer sufficient light, cross ventilation, and air flow through the house?

In new construction, there are formulas to determine how many windows should be in the house based on square footage and design. In an older house, the answer is more subjective, and the decision rests with the homeowner. In an older or historic house, there may be fewer windows because the high cost of glass prohibited the builders in earlier centuries from putting in as many windows as might be put in a home today. Ask yourself the following:

- Can the windows be easily opened and closed on a regular basis?
- Are there enough closets for storing the occupant's clothes and other items? In some older homes, there are either very few or no closets. In this case, closets can be added, or furniture can be purchased to act as storage units.
- Do wall partitions need to be moved?
- Are there enough rooms, or is there a need for an addition?

From the answers to these questions, determine if you are satisfied with the layout of the house. If not satisfied, think about how the space can be altered. Prior to tearing down, building up, or extending the size of the house, consider how the proposed changes will affect the electrical system, plumbing fixtures, aesthetic value, and impact on other rooms in the house.

The following are some tips to keep in mind before beginning to change the floor plan:

- **Permits** — Changing load-bearing walls, pulling down chimneys, or building additions usually requires permits.

- **Layout changes for a historic house** — Become familiar with the guidelines required to alter the home. What building materials can be used? What design changes are acceptable?

- **House knowledge** — Become familiar with the plumbing, heating, and electrical systems. Find out where the load-bearing walls are and where the joists are located.

When making plans, follow these guidelines:

1. Measure rooms.
2. Draw plans.
3. Draw rough sketches.
4. Make sure there is enough room for existing furniture, appliances, and daily activities when creating new spaces.
5. Make a budget.
6. Decide which projects you want to do, and which will need a professional.

Types of Flooring

There are two common floor constructions popular in older homes: the earthen floor and the suspension floor. The main problem with a dirt floor is the excess moisture it creates and the lack of proper ventilation to expel the moisture. It is imperative that moisture problems be resolved prior to the restoration of an existing floor or the installation of new flooring. The suspension floor hangs from the walls, and wood (or steel) joists connect the walls and provide a base to affix the surface floor.

The first step in assessing your flooring needs is to determine the construction of the floor. Second, determine the current condition of the floors and if they are worth keeping. Perhaps the renovations will be done at one time or room-by-room. There is no rule that all rooms need the same flooring. Kitchen and bathroom floors have specific requirements.

In many older homes, there are several layers of flooring. These layers offer a history lesson in flooring materials available throughout the life of the home. Most homeowners would simply add a new layer of flooring on top of what existed instead of removing a layer. Wood planks were the first layer of flooring and then, based upon the times and the homeowner's taste, there might be multiples layers that include linoleum, sheet flooring, or carpeting.

If lucky, there might be a gem of a floor ripe for restoration. Sometimes minor repairs can salvage an original and interesting floor. After figuring out the floor construction, it is time to determine the type of floor that best fits in the home. The following are descriptions and applications of flooring choices:

Wood Flooring

Many homes over 100 years old will have wood planks as the first layer of flooring. The next layer is typically the next generation of wood flooring, which is the strip hardwood flooring. This style of flooring is highly sought after by today's home-buying public. If the wood strips are not water-damaged, buckled, or warped, they can be sanded and brought back to life and enjoyed for many more years. If this layer of flooring is in disrepair, it is best to replace the whole floor. If only some of the strips are damaged, they can be replaced, and the entire floor can be sanded and refinished.

Steps to refinish wood floors

Refinishing wood floors is labor-intensive but rewarding when completed. It is ideal to refinish wood floors when the house is empty. If this is not possible, use large sheets of plastic to seal off the rooms that are not being refinished. This will help to reduce the amount of sand particles in these rooms.

1. Remove any layer or layers of flooring.

2. Repair any defects in the wood prior to refinishing. Make sure all loose boards are nailed down. Remove any nails that are higher than the wood level, or nail them back in.

3. Replace any rotted or greatly damaged boards.

4. Measure the surface of the floors to be refinished.

5. If there is paint on the floors, remove the paint with a commercial paint-removing solution.

6. Buy all stains and sealers prior to renting equipment.

7. Rent sanding equipment from an equipment rental company or home improvement retailer. Be sure to get advice on how to use the equipment before leaving the rental store or company.

8. Go with the grain of the wood when sanding floors. Wear soft-sole shoes to prevent creating any scuffs or additional damages to the newly sanded floors.

9. Vent the area by opening windows and doors. Sanding floors is messy and can have health risks. One of the layers being sanded could be lead paint, so take precautions by wearing safety glasses and a mask.

10. Use a drum sander as your main tool to sand floors. The sandpaper used for a drum sander comes in three grits: coarse (32/0 open grit), medium (60 or 80 grit), and finer (100 grit) papers. Be sure to get some extra sandpaper and belts for the sander. Any extra supplies can be returned with the equipment.

11. Use strength and finesse to operate a drum sander. This is a powerful piece of equipment, and it takes practice to operate it without digging up the floor. It requires a light and quick touch, not a heavy-handed approach. It is important to keep the sander moving at all times. If the sander remains idle on the floor, it will dig into the wood and create deep scars.

12. First, use the coarse sandpaper to get rid of the majority of the soil, deep scratches, and layers of finishing products that have been applied to the floor over the years.

13. Second, go over the floors with the medium-grit sandpaper to get down to a more finished floor.

14. The final step in sanding is to use the fine coarse paper to sand it to the finished and fine look so the wood grain stands out and the major defects have been removed.

15. The next step is to use an edge sander. This sander is used to sand edges and corners, or any other area of floor that the drum sander cannot reach. This is a tedious step because it requires kneeling or bending over to sand edges.

16. There might be spots that neither piece of equipment will reach, so use a piece of sandpaper wrapped around a block of wood to reach those spots.

17. After all the sanding is complete, clean the floor with a good industrial vacuum. The final step is to clean the floor with a tack cloth to pick up sand dust left behind from the vacuum.

18. Apply a stain to the floor if a different color is desired. Follow manufacturer's directions for application steps and drying time.

19. Apply four or five coats of water-based polyurethane to the floors. This will need to be repeated after five years of wear. If there are cracks between the boards, leave some sawdust in the cracks and apply extra sealant in the cracks to seal in the sawdust and make the cracks look less obvious. This will also prevent dirt and dust from getting inside the cracks and making them more difficult to keep clean. All other floors can be coated with three or four coats, and the finish will last for many years to come.

20. Other finishes are available, but polyurethane is the easiest to apply and provides very good results.

Painting on wood floors was a popular technique. The use of stencils and patterns can be used to replicate this historic practice begun in the early 1800s. Prior to stenciling or painting, be sure to add a coat of high-quality marine varnish. A polyurethane finish is not recommended as a base because it is a harder finish. Pine floors and other softwoods are not the best floors to paint or stencil on because of their soft nature; heel marks and heavy traffic will quickly wear out a design.

Tile Flooring

There are many different types of flooring tiles. Traditionally, they were commonly used in just kitchens and bathrooms, but today they are used in every room of the house and outdoor spaces. Tiles come from all parts of the world and can be used for surfaces such as countertops, furniture, walls, and risers for stairs. They only work well when used on a hard, flat, clean, and dry surface, affixed with a thin layer of mortar. The spaces between the tiles are filled with grout.

In older homes, the problems homeowners usually find are loose, dirty, or damaged grout, and cracked or missing tiles. If the tiles are in reasonably good shape, make an effort to try to rejuvenate them. If the grout is intact, try to clean it with a commercially available product from a hardware or home improvement store. If sections of grout are missing or too soiled to be cleaned, then remove and replace the grout.

It is best to remove all of the grout instead of only removing sections and replacing them with new grout. The new grout color will not match the color of the older grout. Removing grout is a tedious and time-consuming process, but well worth the effort. There is a handheld tool that has a small saw blade that is used to remove grout. Once all grout is removed, clean out the cracks between the tiles thoroughly and apply a fresh batch of grout.

Alternatively, if tiles are cracked or missing, they can be difficult to match and replace. Aged and discolored tiles might look fine on the floor, but it might be impossible to find the same tiles in a store or catalog. The only hope is if there are some replacement tiles left in the house from the previous owner. Tiles are made in lots; when working with tile, they should all come from the same lot number.

Over time, tiles discolor and have an aged look, so trying to replace a tile from the same lot might not work. Another solution is to remove several good tiles in a random fashion and replace them with a decorative tile that complements the older tile. Sometimes it is possible to remove all the outer edges of a tile floor and use them to replace the broken tiles. Then, replace the outer tiles with a different tile that creates an attractive border.

Tiles are made from different materials and are used for different applications. They come in different shapes, colors, and thicknesses. The following list details the different types available:

- **Ceramic tiles** — Made of refined natural clay, along with other additives. They can be compressed into many shapes and go through a glazing and firing process. In Victorian days, ceramic tiles were hand-painted. Today, they can still be found this way, but this technique adds to the expense.

- **Quarry tiles** — Similar to ceramic, but they are made from unrefined clays that have not gone through the glazing process; they will need to go through a sealing and polishing process after installed. They come in natural colors like browns, dark reds, and buff.

- **Marble** — Marble is a heavy, natural stone that is an elegant choice, and water will not pass through it. It is expensive option, so it is best used on small floors. Because of its weight, make sure to have a sturdy sub-floor.

- **Mosaic tiles** — Made from ceramic tile, stone, or glass, and are imbedded in a layer of fine mortar. They will usually have a design or depict an image and are an expensive option for flooring. A mosaic insert surrounded by a different type of tile (or other flooring material) is an attractive option for an area like the entranceway into a room, a section of a patio, or in front of a fireplace.

- **Granolithic** — A concrete floor with chips of finely graded granite chips. This type of floor is rough but very durable.

- **Terrazzo** — This is similar to the granolithic flooring, but multi-colored aggregates are inserted into the concrete. After the floor dries, it is smoothed and polished.

- **Bricks** — Although less common for interior spaces, they can work well for hallways, patios, sunrooms, and casual spaces. They are durable and easy to keep clean. An alternative to natural brick is to use a product found in flooring stores that are tiles in the shape and color of brick, but the thickness of other flooring tiles.

- **Natural stones** — These are another flooring material that are durable and come in different colors and shapes. These can readily be identified by where they naturally come from.

Walls

The walls of an older home might require repair, replacement, tearing down, or moving. The original materials used for the walls will reflect the year the house was built.

In planning interior renovations, look at the walls and determine if they need repair, restoration, or replacement. Make these decisions in conjunction with any plans to change floor plans, tear down walls, or add new walls so you do not repair walls that end up getting torn down when a change in the floor plan is being considered.

Types of walls in an older home

Plaster

There is one surefire way to tell if a wall is a plaster wall: Take your thumb and press into the wall. If it gives a little and leaves a small indentation, it is drywall. Plaster is incredibly hard and has a surface durability like no other wall material. The first step in making a traditional plaster wall can still be made today. It begins by nailing thin wood strips known as lath, spaced ½ inch apart to the wall's frame. The next step is to begin to apply plaster in layers.

Three layers are applied. The first layer is a rough plaster comprising more sand than the others. This coat fills the gaps between the lath boards, and the plaster oozes between the spaces in between the strips of wood. Second, a smoothing layer is applied and is made of a finer plaster. The final layer is a smooth, glass-like finished coat. After this layer of glossy finish is applied, the result is a rock-hard glossy wall. There is also a rough, prickly type of final finish plaster that creates a stucco wall that can be applied instead of the glossy finish.

Repairing plaster walls is expensive because it is a lost art, and finding a skilled plasterer is difficult. But minor plaster repairs are done easily enough. Patching plaster and a putty knife will take care of most small cracks. If a section of lath needs to be replaced, it can either be done by nailing in new wooden strips or by affixing a mesh made out of metal over the frame and then applying the plaster.

The installation of plaster walls are more expensive than drywall walls, very durable, more soundproof, and easier to repair and patch. The craft of traditional plastering has enjoyed a distinct renaissance in both high-end new construction and older and historic home renovations and restorations. This increased interest is generated by a desire to complete authentic restorations by preservationists and homeowners who appreciate time-honored techniques that have proved to last over centuries. They are willing to pay extra to have their homes repaired and restored using original materials and techniques to maintain the character and integrity of their homes.

Drywall

Drywall (often called Sheetrock) has been a viable replacement for plaster in price and ease of installation starting around the time of World War II. It is a soft wall material made of a gypsum plaster, sandwiched between two pieces of cardboard. Drywall comes in sheets 8 or 12 feet long and 4 feet wide but can be found longer. Today, it is the most common type of wall covering because it is easy to install, versatile, and affordable.

Installers are not hard to find and are reasonably priced. The worst thing about drywall is how easy it can be damaged. Fortunately, it can be fixed easily by do-it-yourselfers. Small holes and dents can be fixed with a dab of joint compound, a little sandpaper, and a touch of paint. Large repairs require the individual to cut out the damaged area and install a new piece of drywall, filling in the gaps, then applying a smooth layer of joint compound. If the damage is too large, just replace the whole sheet of drywall.

CASE STUDY: TIPS ON DRYWALLING

Terry Wells
Manchester, Tennessee
Drywall Finisher

Terry Wells, a drywall professional in Tennessee, gave a ballpark estimate of the cost of tools for an average-size residential drywall installation: "To do the job professionally and have a home you are proud of, you must use the right tools and equipment. That can run you anywhere from $3,000 to $4,500 to use the most up-to-date equipment," he said.

Drywall is a popular choice for walls over plaster. It is much easier to repair holes in drywall than in plaster. The process is simple, and repairs can be made to the smallest dents or holes a foot wide or bigger.

There are various tools to use when repairing drywall. Most small repairs can be done using a minimal amount of equipment unless extenuating circumstances exist. The most common tools used in drywall repair include:

- Straightedge
- Tape measure
- Joint knives
- Utility knife
- Drill/driver
- Scissors
- Sanding sponge
- Drywall saw
- Dust mask

There are also a variety of materials used in repairing drywall. Before beginning a drywall repair project, assess how much material will be needed and have it on hand. The following materials required:

- Drywall scraps for patches
- Drywall tape
- Drywall screws
- Construction adhesive
- Drop cloth
- Joint compound
- Drywall patching plaster
- Piece of wire screen
- String
- Masking tape
- 1x2 or 1x4 lumber for backer boards

Drywall is relatively soft, and anything pushed hard enough into it will leave a shallow indentation in the wall. Dents are easily repaired to look perfect. Wells recommends using a hot patch for small dents and bangs. "A hot patch is only useful when your hole is 6 to 7 inches in diameter. Anything larger, and it will be sloppy and inefficient," Wells said.

There are three major steps to repairing minor dents in drywall:

1. Dust off loose edges and sand the dent to harden the surface. Dip a joint knife into the compound sideways and place the compound on the blade, up to about half of the blade's thickness. Pull the knife through the depression slowly and with an even stroke. In order to discard excess compound, position the knife at a 90-degree angle and pull across once again. Once dry, the patch may become smaller. If this happens, put on another coat.

2. In order for the fixed spot to blend in with its surroundings, lightly sand it, and use a damp sponge to smooth it.

3. Because they are absorptive, joint compounds need to be primed before painting them. Some paints are also primers.

With appropriate application and timing, patching up drywall can be simple. There is a set order of operations to follow for this process:

1. Using the sharp edge of a knife, carefully peel the edges away to pull off old tape.

2. Before placing the new tape, place compound on the wall and smooth out bubbles with gentle, sideways knife strokes.

3. Apply a second coat when the mixture is still wet. After it dries, put on another lighter coat. Spread the edges, and sand or sponge to complete.

While not as laborious, skills and expertise will determine proper completion for setting popped nails. Press the panel onto the stud, and push new nails above and below the old one. With increased holding power, ring-shank nails are the best to use. Using a last hammer blow, make an indent below the surface of each nail. After pulling out the popped nail, use a joint compound to fill any indentations. Apply a second coat once the compound has dried and thinned. Spread out the edges of the additional coat. After one day, the area can be sponged, primed, and painted.

Small holes in drywall are repaired similarly to small dents or scratches. Gauging the project before beginning is a way to get an idea on what you will need, as well as how long it is going to take to complete the job. Patching small 4- to 6-inch holes in drywall can be an inexpensive task, but it requires patience and skill:

1. Shape the hole into a rectangle by using a keyhole saw and a drywall bandage. Cut the drywall segment into a shape that matches the hole. The cut-up needs to measure 2 inches longer and 2 inches wider than the hole.

2. With the shiny side face down, place the drywall on a flat surface. Make a line starting an inch from all four edges, and a shape about the size of the hole should be created.

3. Cut to the bottom layer of drywall by using a straight edge and utility knife. Avoid cutting this bottom layer. Take a putty knife and carefully take off the top layer until you reach the bottom layer of paper. Make sure not to tear the bottom layer in the process.

4. The cut portion will fit inside the hole, while an inch around the hole will be covered by the paper edge. Place a thin coat of patching compound around the hole. Next, put the patch inside the hole. With a putty knife, carefully add the paper edge to the patching mix. After spreading out the edges of the compound, let it dry. Add a light second coat and sand gently if necessary.

Small holes can be repaired simply by using polymer fabric patches. After cutting them to a preferred size, use an iron set on medium heat and press on the patch. Apply the patching compound to the fabric and allow it to dry for at least 24 hours. Sand with a fine sandpaper to eliminate any lumps, bumps, or uneven streaks in the patchwork.

Patching larger holes is a bit harder and more labor-intensive than small holes or dents. It takes much more skill, as well as physical capabilities:

1. Cut a piece of drywall at least 2 inches larger than the hole to serve as a patch. Puncture the patch with two small holes and tie a stick to it, leaving at least 8 inches of space from the board to the stick.

2. Using high-quality adhesive, cover around the edges of the patching material.

3. Pull the patching board through the hole and place it firmly so the adhesive can form around the outer area of the hole.

4. While turning the stick clockwise, gradually increase pressure on the patch board at the bottom of the hole by twisting the string.

The string will keep the board steady in its place until the adhesive is dry and fully tightened.

5. It is essential to let the adhesive have adequate time to dry. After completely dried, use a high grade of patching plaster to fill the area. Keep the stick and string in the same place throughout this entire patching process.

6. In order to properly patch the area, it may be required to use two or three layers of patching plaster. However, do not apply another layer before one is thoroughly dry.

7. Prior to the patch's being completely dry, the stick and string can be taken out. While waiting for the patch to fully dry, make sure to even out the area.

8. After drying is finished, use fine-grade sandpaper along with a sanding block to smooth out any rough spots. Brush on a prime coat, then apply a final coat of paint.

9. A supporting brace must be used for the patch when there are larger holes in the drywall. A short piece of 2x4 serves as a great supporting brace for patching larger holes. Make sure the pieces of 2x4 expand at least 8 inches past the hole.

10. On one piece of 2x4, place high-quality cement and drive it through the hole. Tie this to another 2x4, making sure it is parallel in front of the drywall.

11. Keep both 2x4 pieces tied for one to two hours, or until the cement is completely dried.

12. After untying the string, take away the front piece of 2x4 that served as a support. Now, the cement will keep the back piece steady in place and also act as a support for the wall patch.

13. Cut out a patch block identical to the area of the sawed-out portion. The hole should be somewhat bigger than this block, and the block should fit as snugly as possible.

14. To cover the hole, apply cement to the back of the patch block and support, and place the patch into position.

15. With a putty knife or patching spatula, distribute joint compound around the drywall patch.

16. Allow the compound to enter into all cracks and scratches. Get rid of extra material by scraping it off, then wait until the patched area dries completely.

17. Smooth tough, elevated areas on the patched surface using a sanding block and fine sandpaper once thoroughly dry. Brush on a prime coat before painting the wall.

Paneling

In older homes, wood paneling was an attractive and distinctive way to finish walls and provide a layer of insulation. The product ranged from very simple designs to more complex, artistically carved wall coverings. The nature of the paneling found in the home will depend on the age and style of the home but will most likely be the real, solid-wood paneling that was characteristic of affluent homes and offices in the 1940s and 1950s, usually made of knotty pine, mahogany, maple, or oak.

Tongue-and-groove boards were also popular wall coverings, found in older and historic homes. These wood planks were machine-enhanced with a tongue on one edge and a groove on the other so they would fit together. These types of planks came in various widths and thickness, and they are still sold today. One of the benefits of using paneling in an older home is that it can cover damaged plaster walls, provide height to a room, and save homeowners money.

In the 1970s, a new form of cheap, thin paneling came into being. Over the years, manufacturing techniques and technologies have generated a mass-produced paneling product. Today, there are thin plywood sheets covered with a wood veneer that provide an affordable and attractive way to cover walls.

Another way to save on costs while still getting the ambience of the solid wood feel is to install wainscoting. Wainscoting panels part of the wall and has a chair-rail molding installed at the top of the panel where chairs are likely to rub and hit the wall. The chair rail protects the wall from damage. Another way to use wainscoting is to make it a little higher than head level and top it with a thick cap rail to display dishes or family heirlooms. Wainscoting is now almost always made of a less expensive material like a processed wood product or a composite material, but it is still attractive and durable.

If paneling is damaged, or another wall treatment is desired, then most paneling can easily be removed, wall condition assessed, and a new wall treatment applied. When walls are in good shape, then a skim coat of plaster can repair any damages left from removing panels. After removing panels, it might be determined that the walls are in poor condition and installing new paneling is a good option, or removing plaster and affixing sheet rock.

CHAPTER 10

Kitchens

The renovation of a kitchen or bathroom can be the most creative, challenging, and expensive phase of the home renovation. Both projects can provide years of enjoyment to the homeowners, and the upgrades can turn into additional financial rewards if the house is sold. It is possible for a homeowner to recoup all or part of their renovation cost, provided the renovations appeal to the potential buyer. Keep in mind that if you spend $75,000 on a kitchen renovation that has red wall tiles, black granite countertops, white cabinets, and gray marble floors, this color scheme may appeal to only a few buyers. Homeowners who plan elaborate designs, colors, and renovations run the risk of not being able to sell their home at a higher price.

If the renovations are done in a neutral color scheme with top-of-the line materials, then potential buyers are more likely to be attracted to the new appliances, quality tile work, modern fixtures, and well-designed spaces. Outdated kitchens and bathrooms can be either a positive or a negative when trying to sell a house because some potential buyers would prefer to make changes that suit their taste.

Kitchen Renovations

The kitchen is usually the busiest room of the house. It has gone from being boring and utilitarian to a bright and active gathering place. Before starting a renovation, think about how a kitchen fits your family's lifestyle. If you have lived in the house for a while, you should make a list of the things that work for you and the things that do not. The goal of the renovation is to right some of the wrongs and improve the room. Here are questions to ask during the initial stage of planning a kitchen renovation:

- Does the current kitchen flow smoothly?

- Do you like the location of the current kitchen? Would it be better to relocate it to another part of the house?

- Is there just one cook in the household, or does more than one person like to participate in meal preparation?

- How much entertaining happens in the house?

- Is an eat-in kitchen important?

- Is there enough storage? Are there enough cabinets? If you buy in bulk, do you need a place to store these extra foodstuffs?

- Is there enough counter space? Is the counter space the right height?

- Do children need a space to do homework?

- Do you want space for a television, computer or a desk? Do you need a place to store cookbooks?

- Is there counter space next to the refrigerator so you can put away groceries or take food out of the refrigerator?

- Is there easy access to the rest of the house?

- Is there too much access through the kitchen? Should a door be eliminated to cut access to the kitchen?

- Is there access to the dining room?

- Would you like to enhance your outdoor space and add a deck off the back of the kitchen? This would be the time to add another door to lead to the outdoors.

- Should the kitchen open up into another adjacent room in the house?

- Does your family eat most of their meals at home, or do they eat out often?

- Are there gourmet cooks in the house? If yes, consider selecting high-end professional appliances.

- Should small appliances be mounted under cabinets, or should they rest on the counter space?

- Is there enough room to open the oven door without banging into an open cabinet door?

- Is it easy to take trash out?

- Is there enough lighting and ventilation?

- Are the current appliances large enough to handle the capacity of the family?

Today's kitchens offer many bells and whistles, but the ability to incorporate them into the design will be influenced by your budget. The following are important ideas and concepts to include in the design of the new kitchen, when the budget allows:

- Use quality materials that will last.

- Buy and install durable building materials and appliances.

- Pick out elements that will stand the test of time instead of buying trendy items.

- Use quality tiles and make sure they are professionally installed.

- Use quality plumbing fixtures.

- Choose an eat-in kitchen, as it is desirable even if in a small area.

- Design a lot of counter space into the new room, especially if there is more than one person cooking at any time.

- Make sure there is plenty of storage space; a pantry is a bonus room that is highly desirable.

- Make sure the traffic flow in the kitchen works smoothly.

- Make sure there is space if family members and guests tend to congregate in the kitchen.

- Make sure islands are suitable for your family. Although islands are in high demand as work and eating surfaces, it might be better to have traditional counter space and a table and chairs, instead.

- Incorporate a desk, computer, and organizational units to modernize your kitchen. This is something to consider if having a place to plan daily activities is important.

Warning!

When renovating a kitchen, it is best if the renovations can be done when the house is empty. Renovating a kitchen while residing in the home creates stress and upheaval for those living in the construction zone. If you are not able to renovate when the house is empty, then plan to set up a separate space in the house for cooking and eating. Plan on simple meals, and use the microwave as much as possible. Renovations usually end up taking more time than planned, so add a few extra days to your original plan.

When planning the new kitchen, take into consideration the following building aspects of the project:

1. Make sure either you or the contractor is familiar with building codes applicable to the project.

2. Apply for the permits and inspections as required.

3. When removing walls, make sure they are not load-bearing. These can be removed, but something else needs to be put in place to carry their original load.

4. Will doors and windows remain where they are, or will they be relocated? Is there easy access to the rest of the house? Windows provide natural light, but if they are being removed or relocated, how will this impact the light in the room? How will this alter the view to the outside?

5. If walls are being removed or added, take into consideration how they impact the rest of the room.

6. Keep in mind plumbing fixtures and pipes and have them replaced or improved, if necessary.

7. Does the demand for electricity require more circuits to be brought to the room? Determine if there are enough electrical outlets and circuits available for the big and small appliances; lighting needs to be bright especially in cutting, cooking, and meal preparation areas.

8. Determine if the heating and cooling sources need to be altered with the design of the new room.

Kitchen safety

A kitchen is a common room in the house for accidents to occur. Follow these safety tips to avoid injuries:

- Store the least-used items at the very top and bottom of cabinets. This avoids the excessive use of step stools and ladders.

- Keep children away from cooking and prepping areas. Have a designated area in the kitchen where they can play, do homework, or watch TV, yet be away from cooking and cutting activities.

- Avoid having electrical wires mix with other items on the counters, such as breadboxes or decorative items, by having enough electrical outlets.

- Do not have several appliances plugged into one outlet or circuit.

- Make sure there is not a draft from windows or doors near the stove to prevent pilots being blown out or curtains blowing near a cooking surface.

- Keep cleaning items safely stored on high shelves instead of under the sink. If the home has small children, childproof the lower cabinets where other kitchen items are stored.

- Keep a fire extinguisher and a first-aid kid nearby.

The Division of Labor and Design

Who will design the kitchen? Who will do the labor? If the room needs painting, new appliances, and cosmetic improvements, most do-it-yourselfers can accomplish these improvements on their own. If the room is to be gutted and transformed into a new, efficient, and modern workspace, will you be able to design it yourself, or will you need to hire a designer or architect? Can you frame in a new wall, install new cabinets, tile a floor, lay new countertops, or install new plumbing?

A major kitchen renovation is a big job, and not for someone who is not able to manage the projects, and do the work. Are you familiar with building codes and how to get permits? In order to get permits, a plan will need to be drawn and presented to the inspection department in the community. Can you draw plans for inspectors and contractors to follow? Are you familiar with kitchen designs and principles? Are you creative at coming up with solutions that are practical and functional? If any changes are made, will they make sense to the building trades? If the home is a historic house, consider finding someone with experience working on these styles.

Hiring professionals to create the plan and do the labor will seem to cost more in the beginning, but could save in the end, especially if things go wrong. Some of the benefits of using professionals such as a designer, architect, contractor, or carpenter are:

- They can manage the project.
- They can draw the plans.
- Professional plans could mean fewer changes mid-stream.
- They know the local codes.
- They know the materials and the resources to get them at a better price.
- They know the structural impact of making changes; they have good planning and schedule skills through experience, and have vision and training.
- They have specific skills to make your dream kitchen a reality.

When hiring a professional, look for the partner who will make the renovation a success. Talk to as many individuals/companies as it takes to make the decision. Use the following tips to help make the decision:

- Ask to see their work portfolio.
- Check out projects they have completed.
- Ask for references and call them.
- Word-of-mouth is the best way to find professionals to take on the renovation.

- Ask them if they have the time to take on the project. Can they give you the time and attention you need?
- Ask about all the costs involved. Will you be paying by the hour, a set fee, or a percent of the project cost?
- Get a contract, read it thoroughly, and understand the terms and conditions.

Designers are not licensed but can bring a great deal of experience and practical know-how to the project. Architects are trained professionals with at least a bachelor's degree in the discipline. They are licensed if they have worked for a registered architect for a set period of time. Once they are licensed, they can become registered, which makes them legally responsible for their work. Carpenters can design and draw plans, too. Through their practical experience, some can bring both trade and design skills. Whether you hire someone or do the work yourself, the kitchen is the toughest room to renovate, so before tearing down anything, have as much planning done as possible.

The Kitchen Triangle Principle

The kitchen triangle is a basic design principle often utilized to help develop an efficient kitchen workspace where people move at a minimum while preparing meals. The three main points of the triangle are the sink, refrigerator and the stove/oven. This concept is a good way to begin a plan for a new kitchen. It is not the only option, but it is a practical and proven plan.

The legs of the triangle connecting the points should be between 4 feet and 9 feet in length in order for the design to work effectively for the cook(s) and the other residents of the home. The total length of all three legs should be between 12 and 26 feet in length. These are rough measurements and can be adjusted according to the needs of the residents.

Kitchen Designs

The following are descriptions of kitchen designs found in most homes that can be used if size and shape permits:

- **The single galley/corridor** — This kitchen is narrow, and the appliances and counter space is on one wall. There is room for the triangle design, cabinets, counter space, and a space to walk, but no room for a dining area. This works well when the kitchen is at least 6.6 feet wide and opens up into another living space where eating and socializing can take place.

- **The double galley** — This kitchen is a good option when the room is at least 7.2 feet wide and working units are placed along each wall. The area needs to be wide enough to accommodate two people passing each other in the open space and to allow occupants room to bend down to get things from cabinets and the refrigerator. This layout does not work well when there are doors to break up the flow of the counters.

- **The peninsula** — This layout is a work surface that projects into the room at a right angle and can be used as a work surface or eating area, or both. It offers a counter with cabinets below that can be constructed so they can be reached from both sides of the peninsula. This feature can conveniently divide a room and offer separation where most needed. When looking into this workstation, consider if having a permanent room divider is the desired effect, or if an island or dining table offer the same result.

- **The U-shape** — This kitchen is comparable to the double galley layout where the triangle is in a U-shape, and at the other end is an area to place a dining table. Doors and windows will influence where to put appliances.

- **The L-shape** — This kitchen is one of the most popular layouts because it needs less floor space and allows the use of islands and workstations. It is well suited when there is an open floor plan and the kitchen opens to a casual area. The kitchen is placed in the corner of a square-shaped room. An island or a dining table can be placed in the open area of this layout.

- **The G-shape** — This kitchen is similar to the L-shape unit, but is smaller and has a sink and stovetop.

The One-Wall Design

If the kitchen space is small, a one-wall design is an alternative to the Triangle design. This is where all the appliances are up against one wall. There will be minimal counter space.

Islands

The installation of an island in today's kitchen has almost become a standard design feature when the room is large enough to handle one. They are a versatile and multipurpose workstation that enhances the kitchen's existing work and cooking surfaces. The size, shape, and functional features are up to the individual. Possible uses include additional food preparation surfaces, storage areas, eating and seating areas, and places to install cooking elements, and sinks.

They work well in the L-shape kitchen and are often used as a room divider between the kitchen and another room. They work well in an open floor plan. Islands require space, and it is best to have one that is at least 10 feet by 10 feet and incorporates many functional features. If this is too big, a smaller workstation will work as long as appliances and cabinet doors open without hitting the island.

Cabinets

If an older home has existing kitchen cabinets that are solid in their construction, have enough storage space, and are the right configuration, they can be refurbished with refinishing and resurfacing techniques.

Applying a coat of paint or a stain to the surfaces can bring cabinets back to life. If you choose this option, make sure the cabinets are clean and free of grease. Lightly sand the surfaces if they are rough, but this is not necessary. If cabinets have been painted with an oil-based paint, use an oil-based paint again.

If you decide to re-stain the cabinets, remove the existing finish first. Sand the surface and apply a commercial chemical stripping product. It is well worth painting or staining the inside of the cabinets, too. Some skip this step, but they are looked at every day, so it is nice to finish them off. They do not have to be painted as perfectly as the outside, but a good layer of the same or different color will be attractive.

If the cabinets need additional renovating, they can be resurfaced. This involves keeping the existing framework and replacing the flat surfaces with new wood, veneers, or laminate materials. Solid wood cabinet doors can be refitted with glass fronts for a new and updated look. Adding hardware to cabinets that have been refinished or resurfaced is the last step involved in sprucing up the existing cabinets in either the kitchen or bathroom.

The next, more expensive option is to replace the cabinets. When replacing cabinets, there are a few options available:

1. Buy ready-made cabinets.

2. Have new cabinets custom-made to accommodate the resident's tastes in wood that finishes the home's space configurations. Choose features such as a lazy Susan, deep drawers, recycling bins, slide-out

drawers and shelves, and other cabinet features that make finding items easier.

3. When ordering cabinets, take accurate measurements to make installation easier. This is a crucial step, so measure two or three times, and get guidance from the seller and manufacturer on how to measure for a particular product. Mistakes are often made by not measuring correctly to allow for protruding walls, or not taking into consideration the need to match corners. It might be worth a small fee to have a service person take the measurements. If there are errors, they will be responsible.

Ready-made cabinets

Ready-made cabinets can be found at large home improvement retailers and smaller cabinet shops. They are manufactured in many styles, wood materials, and surface finishes. They have numerous features a consumer can choose from that are a major improvement from cabinets found in older homes. The height of the typical cabinet is 35 inches, but they can be custom-made with features for those who are very tall or short, or for those who are elderly or disabled.

If buying ready-made cabinets, make sure to look them over closely. Compare different manufacturers, prices, and features. Most retailers will have display units on the floor so consumers can see how the cabinets will look once installed. Paying to have cabinets installed is costly, so choose ones that will last and will not have to be replaced. Cabinets that are made with inexpensive materials and shoddy construction will need to be replaced sooner.

Check the interior and exterior to determine if they are the best choice. The framework boxes can come in different materials. Solid-wood cabinets are top-of-the-line and the most expensive; plywood is in the moderate price range; and composite materials are the least expensive. Be sure to look at the materials and how the drawers are constructed. Do not hesitate to pull out a drawer and check over the construction.

Grab a few items in the store that have some weight; put them in the drawer and see how well the drawer functions. Do the shelves have notches so they can be adjusted according to your needs? Do you like the hardware, or are there other options you can choose from?

The type of wood and finishes available for cabinets varies. Decisions on this choice will depend on individual taste and budget. If trying to choose period styles to match the age of the home, then choose wood, styles, and finishes to keep pace with the time when the home was built. If the cabinets are ready in boxes to be purchased and brought home, then they are ready for installation.

Some products will need to be ordered, so determine when delivery date is expected. Can cabinets be delivered directly from the manufacturer to your door? What are delivery costs? What are installations costs? What are the guarantees, if any?

Custom-made cabinets

Custom-made cabinets open up the possibilities when it comes to style, features, materials, and finishes. This is the more expensive option, but cabinets usually remain in the home for decades, so getting what you want is sometimes worth the extra expense. Shop around for price and quality, and compare all costs and features available before ordering. The top-of-the-line cabinets will come with a hefty price, but the craftsmanship and options available will be enjoyed every day.

Before ordering custom-made cabinets, understand the guarantees and the seller's responsibility if repairs are required. Always have the seller measure the space and listen to their suggestions on the layout. The final decision comes from the consumer, but those in field have an expertise that is worth listening to. Find out what the return policy is, if returns are allowed.

No matter whether the cabinets are custom- or ready-made, they will need to be installed, and this is something a handy homeowner can do. It is not a technical project, but it does require some basic construction skills. Ready-made cabinets will offer installation instructions from the manufacturer, so read the instructions carefully.

It is helpful to have help from someone who is strong and in good physical condition to help hold cabinets in place. For a fee, the large retail home building supply companies will do the installation when the product is purchased from them. Determine the price of installation and if there is a delivery or shipping fee so it can be added into the budget.

Storage

Evaluate the amount of storage in the current kitchen and determine if it is adequate. Storage areas can be shelves, cabinets, furniture, appliances, pantries, or custom-built units. The selection possibilities are endless, and a kitchen can offer storage options such as hooks, racks, plate racks, metal racks, drawers, and brackets.

If the home is historic, consider using a piece or two of antique furniture such as a pie safe or an armoire for storage. Appliances such as deep freezer and a large refrigerator make good storage areas. If you shop in bulk, a deep freezer might be a good choice. Try and make storage units convenient and in close proximity to where you will have access. Do you have a utility room that storage units can be placed in or a pantry that offers additional storage space? Are there spaces in the house that can be converted into closets or storage areas?

Countertops and Work Surfaces

When it comes to countertops and work surfaces, there are many choices. Take into consideration personal preferences, period of the house, budget, and practicality when deciding. Do not forget the backsplash when making countertop choices. A backsplash is the area behind the sink and stove that is covered with a nonporous material to protect the walls from water, grease, and dirt.

The size of the backsplash might be dictated by the existing space or, if there is room, it can be expanded. Homeowners can become creative with the backsplash area and create an eye-catching decorative focal point for the stove and sink areas. Here are some of the more popular choices in kitchen surfaces:

Wood surfaces

Not many consumers choose a wood countertop and work surface, but for those who like the look of wood, butcher block continues to be a good choice because it is tough and manages stains, burns, cuts, and bruises with more fashion than most other surfaces. It can also be sanded and resealed to look like new. Other choices in wood include cherry, maple, mahogany, birch, and pine. Butcher block must be sealed properly to protect it from moisture and water damage.

Laminate

Many patterns and colors are available for this type of countertop surface. Although a laminate surface is easy to clean up, it can be marred by scratches and burns, which cannot be repaired.

Stone

A very sturdy and attractive countertop material is one made out of granite, marble, and soapstone. The hard nature of these natural surfaces does make them attractive and almost indestructible, but the nature of these counters can readily allow them to absorb liquids.

Solid surfaces

These surfaces come in many colors and patterns. They are synthetic and made out of resin. They are popular because scratches can be buffed out, but they can be damaged by knife marks.

Ceramic tile

Ceramic tile is popular and available in many colors, shapes, textures, and sizes. In today's kitchen, the backsplash and the countertop include tile to provide a decorative and waterproof surface. An epoxy grout should be used to fill the gap between tiles; seal the grout with a waterproofing product to keep grout lines easy to clean. Tiles can always be re-grouted if age and dirt have taken their toll. This is a tedious project, so properly sealing the grout lines is well worth the extra effort.

Metal

Metal countertops, like those made of stainless steel, are water- and heat-resistant, and require minimal maintenance. They are simple to clean and affordable, but metal countertops have their downsides. Although the price of steel is relatively inexpensive, the fabrication of the countertop can get pricey. Steel thickness is measured in gauges. Be sure to get at least 16-gauge stainless steel for countertops — thicker, if the budget allows. Other specialty metals such as copper and zinc make beautiful countertops, but they must be polished and maintained regularly in order to prevent dents and scratches.

Concrete

Concrete countertops are easy to clean and practically indestructible, plus they can be ordered in many colors, sizes, and shapes. They arrive ready to install and can accommodate any kitchen countertop, and they come complete with holes for the sink. Concrete can also be poured and finished right at the job site. Concrete countertops are heavier than the average countertop and will require special braces for more support. They have a shiny surface as a result of many passes with a trowel. This is a job for the professionals because of the extensive labor and skill involved. Make absolutely sure that a concrete countertop is what you want, because they are difficult to remove.

Kitchen Sinks and Faucets

Sinks and faucets are some of the finishing touches that require careful consideration. Try not to buy cheap, low-quality products that will cost you money later if they cause leaks or have to be repaired. The sink and faucet are two of the most heavily used fixtures in a kitchen, so it is best not to skimp on these fixtures.

Sinks

Kitchen sinks come in many shapes, colors, and sizes. They are available in up to three bowls, but it is best to choose at least two bowls. Double and triple bowls come with a garbage disposal and a cutting board installed. The most popular kitchen sink arrangements are the single, large rectangular basin; the double-bowl sink with both sides for washing and rinsing; and the double-bowled sink with one side smaller with an accompanying garbage disposal. In today's kitchen, there might be more than one location that has a sink. Kitchen islands can have a sink mounted to their surface.

The standard depth for a sink is 8 inches. Less expensive sinks are 6 or 7 inches deep; 10 inches is the preferred size, which makes it easy to wash large pots, pans, and roasters. Sinks do much more than supply water and a drain. They also facilitate the installation of water purifiers, garbage disposals, soap dispensers, and faucets.

The configuration of the sink will determine how it should be mounted. The following are the three ways they can be mounted:

1. Self-rimming sinks have a lip that overhangs on the surface of the countertop. Sinks can be placed inside a cutout in the counter with a lip that overlaps the counter or under-mounted to the bottom of the counter with metal clips. The biggest complaint with self-rimming sinks is that food and water can get trapped under the rim, causing difficulty in cleaning and some damage to the countertop.

2. An integral sink is a continuation of the countertop. The biggest advantage of an integral sink is it is seamless, so there is no rim to ensnare food, dirt, and water. There are also integral-bowl sinks that are a sleek and seamless unit molded directly in with the counter. They are made of the same material as the counter and form a unique, unspoiled look. There is no chance of water or food gathering under the lip, so cleanup is a snap. The biggest complaint with integral-bowl sinks is that they are shallow.

3. Under-mount sinks feature sink bowls that fuse to the bottom side of the counter. They cannot be used with laminate countertops, but they work well with solid surfacing, stone, or stainless-steel countertops. Under-mounted sinks are more expensive with their sleek look and easy cleanup.

Consider the style and décor of the kitchen and the type of countertop when choosing a sink. Sinks can be made out of the following materials:

Stainless steel

A stainless-steel sink offers restaurant-quality durability. The reason restaurants choose stainless-steel sinks is because of their ability to resist the harm of abrasive cleaners, defy stains, and take a beating without showing a dent. The thickness of stainless steel is measured in gauges. The lower number gauge the steel is, the thicker and stronger the sink is. An 18-gauge stainless steel sink is considered good, but a 16 gauge is better, and a 12 gauge is even better. The downside to stainless-steel sinks is that that they are loud when water is running into them.

Enameled cast iron

Enameled cast-iron sinks come in a myriad of colors, are shiny, and clean up easily. These sinks are not as noisy as steel, but they can chip if hit with a large, heavy object, like an iron skillet or weighty pan. Enamel-on-cast-iron sinks look just like enamel on steel, but are stronger and more fashionable. The considerable weight of a cast-iron sink necessitates sturdy counters.

Vitreous china

Vitreous china sinks are most often found in the bathrooms of older homes. But homeowners are buying them for the kitchens because of their designer looks. They are often etched or painted with intricate, often handmade designs. Their purpose is more ornamental than functional. This type of sink is a poor choice for a kitchen, but it could be used with an island to add a decorative touch to the kitchen. It resists stains and scratches but chips easily.

Solid surface

A solid-surface sink is a two- or three- bowl sink that is manufactured as a one-piece bowl. They can be a self-rim or an under-mount, but this is not the norm. They are made from any of the standard sink materials and carry with them the qualities of those materials. Solid-surfacing sinks are rimless and seamless because they fuse to the adjacent solid-surfacing counter. Solid-surfacing sinks are more expensive than metal and must be installed by a professional.

Specialty metals

Copper makes a stunning sink. A deep, rich color that draws the eye, it also tarnishes and must be dried and polished after each use; brass is the same way. Striking and unmatched in beauty, they are high maintenance. Consider using one of these specialty metal sinks for a secondary sink.

Faucets

How many times a year does the water faucet in the kitchen or bathroom get turned on? Thousands? Millions? Only a solid-brass fixture will allow the strength and durability needed to last through the years. Make sure a kitchen faucet is an all-brass faucet that is heavy for its size. Older homes will have washers in the faucets, but today's homeowners prefer low-maintenance features.

Another timesaving convenience is the ceramic disk valves. They regulate the temperature and flow of the water without deteriorating or dripping, but cost more. Single-lever faucets have one handle that controls both the hot and cold water, and they have one spout. They are best in the kitchen because they can be adjusted with one hand; they are a little pricier than the units with a spout between two handles. It is not unheard of to see a kitchen with the two-handle unit on a single base unit with a separate hot and cold handle and a spout between them. Other amenities to be placed near the faucet are a sprayer, an instant hot water dispenser, a water filter, or soap dispenser.

Kitchen faucets come in different finishes, such as brushed chrome, brushed bronze, brushed nickel, polished chrome, polished brass, copper, antique brass, black iron, and powder-coated enamel. Polished chrome is the most common. It is strong, durable, and versatile because it fits into any kitchen décor.

Kitchen faucets cost $80 to $800 or more, depending on the material and functionality. With faucets, price is an accurate indicator of worth. For example, expect to pay at least $150 for a ceramic disk faucet with solid brass machinery.

Installing a kitchen faucet is a simple job, if you have done your homework. Here are a few items you need to change the faucet:

- New faucet
- Locking pliers
- Adjustable wrench
- Slip joint or water pump pliers
- Basin wrench
- Utility knife
- Plumber's putty or silicon caulk
- Flashlight
- Water supply lines and Teflon® tape

The following are some simple steps to install a faucet:

1. Shut off the water. Many people forget this step, only to be abruptly surprised by a face full of cold water. Close off the shut-off valve under the sink or shut off the main water supply to the house.

2. Disengage the hot and cold water lines under the sink by using an adjustable wrench to loosen the coupling attaching the lines to the faucet.

3. Remove the old bottom-mounted faucet from the top of the sink by taking out the screws inside the faucet handles. Removing the decorative handles reveals the screws. Once you have revealed the screws, remove them. Removing top-mounted faucets are a bit trickier because they require getting under the sink to remove the bolts. Sometimes pipes are in the way; in that case, use a slip joint or water pump pliers so the faucet can be removed without removing pipes. Another tool to use in tight spots is a basin wrench. After the nuts are removed, the faucet can simply be lifted up off the sink.

4. When caulking sticks to the faucet, use a putty knife and run it around the base. This will remove the seal created by the caulking.

5. Once the faucet and caulking is removed, you will find buildup or "gunk" left. This surface must be completely clean in order for the new faucet to fit correctly. Use a mixture of water and vinegar to break down the gunk and clean the surface. You could also use a citrus cleaner and silicone remover from any home improvement store.

6. Then you are ready to install the new faucet. Bottom-mounted faucets are installed by putting them in place and hand-tightening the nuts and washers. When you are sure you have the faucet lined up correctly with the back of the sink, tighten the connections with a wrench. Before installing the escutcheon and faucet handles, first use the silicone caulking around the faucet's base.

7. To install a top-mounted faucet, the process is similar. For this procedure, apply the bead of plumber's putty or silicon caulk prior to placing the faucet in the sink opening.

8. After the connection is properly established between the faucet and the sink, re-install the water feed lines and put the water on. Make sure there are no leaks between the shut off valve and faucet. To avoid hardening of putty or silicon caulk, clean the area with a moist rag.

9. To be cautious, allow the tap water to run for a few minutes by removing the aerator. There are often remnants of the manufacturing process left in the faucet, and running the water will flush them out.

Flooring

The kitchen flooring needs to be sturdy to meet the demands of this high-traffic room. The material needs to be water-resistant, with the ability to be washed regularly to keep the floor free from debris, bacteria, and dirt. When putting in a new floor, there may be several layers of older floors to be removed. Use caution when removing older vinyl floors because the adhesive might contain asbestos. A flooring sample can be tested if asbestos is suspected. If it tests negative, then proceed to remove the flooring. If the test is positive, hire a professional asbestos removal contractor.

When the home is occupied by an active family, then choose a durable floor. A delicate floor is more suitable for one or two adults with limited traffic flow, pets, and cooking activities. The following are descriptions of different varieties of kitchen flooring:

Linoleum

Linoleum is durable and made out of natural products. It is easy to install and available in many colors and patterns. Although often mistaken for vinyl, linoleum is actually a mixture of recycled, earth-friendly products such as wood chips, cork, and plant by-products.

Linoleum's color goes completely through to its underside and enables the homeowner to repair cuts and scrapes effortlessly. Installation is fairly simple and can be done by do-it-yourselfers. However, the sub-floor needs to be smooth to avoid ripples in the finished job. If the sub-floor is not smooth, then consider removing and replacing it. If it is made out of 4- by 8-foot plywood, then perhaps only a few boards will need to be replaced to resolve the problem.

Removing a sub-floor is fairly easy and only requires basic tools, like a pry bar and hammer, to lift up the nails holding the plywood in place. Linoleum is known for its ease of care and durability, which is the reason it is often used in hospitals, schools, and public buildings.

Solid ceramic and porcelain tile floors

Solid tile flooring is one of the most popular materials to use on a kitchen floor. They come in different base materials and are made all around the world. There are ceramic tiles, which are made out of clay and fired and glazed at the manufacturer. There are porcelain tiles that are similar to ceramic tiles, but the color of the tile runs through the whole height of the tile, not just on the surface.

This becomes a factor if the tile chips. The chip is less obvious because the color is same. Quarry tiles are made out of clay but are not glazed, so they will need to be sealed to protect the tiles from dirt, grease, and moisture. These are often found in homes in the West, Southwest, and Florida. Some are reasonably priced and with minor education can be easily installed.

Marble floors

Marble floors are a luxurious addition to any home. They are durable and resistant to stains and water. They come in squares or tile shapes with different thicknesses, and they are heavy, so make sure there is a strong sub-floor beneath them. They are more practical in smaller rooms because they are expensive. Installing marble is similar to installing tile, but due to the expense of the material, it might be wise to have a professional handle the installation.

Vinyl floors

This flexible material comes in many textures, styles, and colors. The material is the next generation in linoleum flooring and is made from polyvinyl chloride (PVC). There are self-sticking, 12-inch vinyl tiles sheets that can adhere to an existing floor as long as it has been thoroughly cleaned, degreased, and repaired. It also comes in 6- to 13-feet-wide rolls. To add extra cushion in the kitchen, make sure to get a vinyl that has a cushion backing to alleviate noise and increase standing comfort.

Cork

Cork is a natural flooring choice that is ideal for kitchens, bathrooms, and children's rooms. It comes in tiles or planks and is durable for normal traffic, yet soft and springy to prevent falling objects from breaking. It is best to choose one that is more expensive and of a better quality.

There is less expensive cork flooring products available, but they are less durable over time. They are easy to install, but make sure the sub-floor is smooth, and follow the manufacturer's installation recommendations. One tip is to make sure to butt the individual tiles or planks closely together to keep water or liquids from seeping between the seams. After installation, coat the cork with some type of acrylic or polyurethane coating, if the tiles did not come sealed. Cork floors will sustain damage easier than other types of flooring, but can easily be repaired.

Wood floors

Many older and historic homes will have the original wood plank floors or hardwood floors that can be restored. These floors have survived the wear and tear of decades of use and are often prized treasures when found by homeowners. Wood floors in a kitchen are practical when they are properly sealed and a suitable finish is applied. New hardwood floors are usually the most expensive option. Softwoods can be used, but they are not as durable.

Wood floors are highly regarded by those who have them, but wood floors are not always feasible in an area where there is water, plumbing, and lots of cooking. Leaks and food spills can make this option impractical, but with the right circumstances and lifestyle this is a great choice. For instance, when there is a minimal amount of activity in the kitchen, then a wood floor is more practical. However, if the kitchen is a very active room with many children in the household, then a wood floor is not as practical. The more cooking and number of residents increases the amount of use of water in and around the sink, and possible grease spills around the stove.

Carpeting

Carpeting is a poor choice in a kitchen because it is difficult to keep clean and free of food and the bacteria. It is best kept for other parts of the house. Area and scatter rugs can be placed in the entranceway(s) to protect floors from moisture and dirt. They can also be placed under a dining table or in front of the sink or stove for decorative purposes and to protect floors from food and grease generated from cooking and eating.

Lighting

Lighting is one feature of a kitchen that can easily be overlooked during the design phase. Combine different types of lighting such as ambient, task, decorative, and accent to offer interest and functionality to the room. The sink area, cooking surfaces, and under-cabinet areas need special attention when it comes to lighting. If there is a desk area in the kitchen or an area where cookbooks and recipes are read, then additional lighting will be welcome.

Ventilation

Make sure an exhaust fan is installed in the kitchen to minimize cooking odors and moisture created from food preparation. It is ideal to have the exhaust fan vented directly out through the roof. If this is not a feasible route for the fumes, then vent the exhaust into the attic (if the attic is not used as a living space). There are also exhaust fans that require no venting and might be the only option available for the space. Microwave ovens that are installed above a stove may come with an exhaust fan, and these may or may not come vented.

Appliances

By the time a kitchen renovation is close to being completed, the budget is usually depleted. If the appliances have not been purchased, then there is a tendency to choose inexpensive ones. But this is not the best approach because major appliances should last for a decade or more. It is a good idea to select appliances at the beginning of the project and select good-quality models.

It is also important to know the dimensions of the appliances so they will fit properly once they are put in place. Once upon a time, buying appliances meant making a choosing between white, yellow, or avocado-green colors. Today's main choices still include the standard white, but black and stainless steel are other standard finishes. Stoves, refrigerators, microwaves, and dishwashers offer products with basics functionality to those operating with all the bells and whistles. There are features to save you space, time, and money; it is certainly not all about color anymore.

AVERAGE LIFE EXPECTANCY OF HOUSEHOLD APPLIANCES	
Stove/range	15-16 years
Refrigerator	13 years
Dishwasher	11 years
Garbage disposal	10 years

Stoves

Stoves operate with electricity or gas, or a combination of the two. The average size for a stove is 30 inches wide, but they come in wider and smaller sizes in order to fit specific kitchen spaces. Commercial ranges are another option and are enjoyed by those who love to cook. They are on average 48 inches wide or wider.

Stoves can come in the following style:

- **Freestanding** — This style can be placed anywhere in the kitchen triangle, as long as there is a power source. There is a cooking top and two finished sides. The back of the stove is unfinished and is placed against a wall, or it fits into another unit like a cabinet that will hide the back.

- **Slide-in** — This style is made to slide in between other appliances and has no finished side panels.

- **Drop-in** — This style does not have finished side panels and is made to drop in and sit on top of a surface. Unlike slide-in models, it has no gaps between appliances.

The electrical or gas hookup in the kitchen might dictate placement. Some prefer a separate cooktop surface and separate oven. The prices will vary according to the jobs each stove performs. Most have a self-cleaning function, but might also have smooth-top electric burners and electric touch controls.

The least expensive stoves will cost around $400, but a stove with features like a circulating oven fan and dual-fuel capacity can easily run $1,500 or more. Dual-fuel ranges are thought to be superior to all others because of their ability to cook with gas on the stovetop and electricity in the oven. These types of ranges will also have special amenities, such as browning features and bread rising options.

Dishwashers

Dishwashers today are not the clanking, clattering contraptions available in the past. Today's models are exceedingly quiet because of added insulation. They are more energy-efficient because they use fewer kilowatt-hours, less water per wash cycle, and air-dry alternatives that do not involve heat. Other energy cost-cutters includes models with internal water heating. These models increase temperatures to levels that will dissolve grease and minimize demands on a home's hot water heater.

Portable dishwashers are also an option, but built-in models are best for a renovated kitchen. Built-in dishwashers can be cleverly disguised behind cabinetry panels, and high-end machines have electronic touch-pad controls, temperature controls, stainless-steel interiors, and wash cycles for crystal, china, and pots/pans. Cheaper, basic models make use of push buttons or combine a dial with buttons. These model types offer three washing cycles: light, normal, and heavy.

Refrigerators

The refrigerator is one of the few appliances that must run continuously; therefore, it is important to pick the right one. The refrigerator's energy conservation feature has made great strides in recent years, especially since mandated standards were set in 1993 and again in 1998. They have also made vast improvements in convenience. However, the basic refrigerator is still available with either 18 or 20 feet of storage and has adjustable shelving and a meat keeper with temperature control. Other options include vegetable crispers with humidity control, icemakers, and wider door bins.

Newer models have at least a 22-cubic-foot capacity. Their side-by-side design with water-and-ice-capable "convenience centers" in the door add extra expediency. For a lush, elegant look, or serious, high-volume storage, choose a built-in refrigerator/freezer or a commercial, stainless-steel model.

A helpful guideline in deciding which size is best for your home is to plan on 12 cubic feet to serve two people and 2 more cubic feet for each additional person living in the house. There are other considerations, such as whether you stock up during sales or cook for crowds on a regular basis. Side-by-side models are super simple to systematize, but these models usually have smaller freezers. Make sure the type of refrigerator you buy can hold your favorite frozen pizza and a ham. Look for pullout bins, rollout baskets, and other amenities that make finding foods easier.

Kitchen refrigerator renovations often go beyond the main fridge. A fun trend is to include a separate under-counter refrigerator for soft drinks and bottled water. A wine fridge is an entertaining option also finding its way into today's kitchens. Another option is to install an icemaker that fits into the space of a trash compactor and will produce larger amounts of ice at one time.

CHAPTER 11

Bathrooms

Renovating Bathrooms

The cost of renovating a bathroom is usually the second-most costly room to improve — the kitchen is typically the most expensive to upgrade. To begin with, determine if the home has enough bathrooms. Decide if it is better to renovate the existing bathroom(s) or build a new bathroom. Many older homes were built with only one bathroom. The addition of a new bathroom increases the value of the home and improves the lives of the occupants.

These days, it is virtually impossible to live with just one bathroom when more than one or two people reside in the home. When building a new bathroom, it is important to place it in a convenient and accessible location for residents. Avoid putting it in a space just because the space is available.

Put the bathroom in an area that makes sense for the residents and is near existing plumbing lines. Moving plumbing lines any distance is costly. Remember this when renovating an existing bathroom, too. To save, replace old bathroom fixtures with new ones, and put them in the same location as before.

The renovation of an existing bathroom or building a new one requires planning, so consider the following points when making decisions on either project:

- Are there enough bathrooms in the house to accommodate the residents?

- Is the layout pleasing?

- Is there an electrical outlet in the bathroom? Does it have a ground-fault circuit interrupter (GFCI)? This is required by the building code.

- Is the water pressure adequate?

- Does the hot water tank provide enough hot water for showers and baths for more than one person? If not, consider getting one with a larger capacity.

- Is there mold in the existing bathroom? This could mean there is excess moisture in the room.

- Is there a ventilation system in place? If yes, does it do a sufficient job of keeping the moisture removed from the bathroom?

- Are tiles falling out? This could mean there is water seeping into the walls from showers or plumbing fixtures. This is a sign that the walls behind the tiles are wet or damp.

- Are there leaks with any of the fixtures? This can increase water bills and promote the development of moisture.

- Does the hardware, such as towel racks, bars, and hooks, accommodate the requirements in the current bathroom? Do you need more, or a different style?

- Is there any countertop space? Is it adequate?

- Is the lighting sufficient?

- Is there anyone in the home who requires handicap features in the bathroom, such as grab rails and a raised toilet?

- Is there enough storage in the bathroom? Is there a linen closet nearby? If storage is required, how can additional capacity be incorporated into renovation plans?

- Is there anyone in the home that requires handicap features in the bathroom such as grab rails and a raised toilet?

- Do the floors sag? This could mean there are leaks and the wood has deteriorated. This could result if the floor is not able to support the weight of the fixtures in the bathroom, such as a toilet or tub.

> **What is a GFCI?**
>
> A GFCI is also known as a ground-fault circuit interrupter and is an extra safety feature found in a home that is in addition to circuit breakers. Building codes require GFCI circuit breakers be installed in bathroom outlets. They are also required in kitchens. When an outlet is located within 4 feet from a sink, a GFCI is required. If an outlet serves a countertop, a GFCI is also needed. Outdoor outlets used near a swimming pool, hot tubs, and some garage outlets require them as well.

- Is there a locked medicine cabinet?

- Are there enough mirrors?

- Is there a window or windows that need fixing? If there is no window in the room, should one be installed?

- Do I need a new bathroom door?

- What is my budget?

- Will I do the work myself or hire a professional?

- What are the building codes relevant for renovating a bathroom?

In the planning phase of a bathroom renovation, there are some nice features to include that will add value and convenience to today's home. The following are modern options to incorporate into the renovation, if the budget and space allow:

- Double sinks
- Spa tubs

- Hot tubs (these require special plumbing and pipes)
- A stall shower and a soaking tub
- A water-saving toilet
- Good-quality hardware and fixtures
- Good-quality tile for floors and walls
- New towel fixtures and racks
- Towel-warming rack
- Wall-mounted power spray heads for the shower

Fixtures

Pipes, plumbing practices, venting, and electrical requirements in bathrooms are behind the scenes and will be dictated by building codes. The fun part is picking out the fixtures, which come in a variety of styles, colors, and shapes. Always try to buy quality products. The up-front costs of quality fixtures might seem prohibitive, but the savings could be substantial later.

The age of the home will dictate the type of fixtures found in the existing bathroom. Is there a claw-foot tub that can be restored? Is there a toilet with a water box attached to the wall? The homeowner must decide if they want to try to restore any of these older fixtures, or replace them with reproductions. It is important to have fixtures that can operate efficiently on a daily basis and will not leak or create plumbing nightmares. If older fixtures create problems now, it is best to replace them.

Bathtubs

If the bathtub is in good shape, you can choose to resurface or paint it in order to spruce it up. If it does not have a shower feature, one can be added along with a new faucet. The wall around the tub can be refurbished with acrylic surrounds or tiles. If the tub needs replacing and you want to keep the same style, then it is worth checking antique shops or junkyards for replacements.

Manufacturers make reproductions of older styles, too. There are many shapes and sizes of tubs available, these days. Bathtubs are free-standing, such as a claw-foot tub, or can be built into or framed into an alcove or corner. There are four main materials to choose from when it comes to a bathtub. The following is a description of each material:

- **Enameled cast iron** — This is a very heavy material that is found in many traditional bathrooms. Although expensive, it is very durable and lasts for many years. It will chip if it is hit with a heavy object.

- **Enameled steel** — This is similar to the cast iron material, but is lighter, less expensive, easier to install, but still very strong and durable.

- **Acrylic** — This is the least expensive material to select for a bathtub. It is light and easy to install, but it is not as strong as others listed above, and it will scratch. Follow manufacturer's recommendations for proper cleaning methods to avoid scratching.

- **Fiberglass-reinforced plastic** — This is made from cast acrylic sheets reinforced with both a fiberglass and polyester resin. This material is used to make many of the molded, shaped tubs and showers. A custom shape can be made of fiberglass, too.

When purchasing a new tub, make sure it will fit through the doorway. This is a mistake many homeowners make when replacing an existing tub. Measure all the doorways the tub will travel through before it reaches its place of installation. The same goes for getting the old tub out.

In many older houses, the tub was installed before doorways were installed. Make sure whatever tub is selected has a non-skid surface to prevent falls.

When installing grab bars and handholds, make sure they are attached wall studs for safety and security.

Showers

Having both a bathtub and a stall shower in a bathroom is a luxury, but today's homeowner looks as a bathroom as a place to relax, so if space is available, they will install both. The alternative is to have at least a bathtub combined with a shower fixture. There are many different ways to approach the installation of a shower unit. Pre-molded units are available, or one can purchase new faucets and a showerhead and create a stall shower by building walls using tile, laminate surfaces, or other waterproof materials.

Make sure the floor has a non-skid surface to prevent falls. If soap dishes, ledges, or other shelves are added, make sure they drain properly so water will not build up.

Showers typically come in either metal or fiberglass. They can be custom-made or purchased in standard sizes. Stall showers come in various configurations such as a molded unit with the walls, floor and ceiling in one piece. If made of fiberglass, they are molded as one piece; if it is metal, they will have seams.

Some showers are sold in pieces to assemble in the bathroom. They include the floor, the walls, and a drain mechanism. No matter which style is purchased, make sure it will fit through doorways and into the bathroom. When shopping for a new shower, check out the features prior to purchasing. Some have handrails, soap dishes, seats, and ledges already incorporated into the mold. Showers have either glass doors or shower curtains. Follow the manufacturer's cleaning recommendations to prevent scratches or discolorations.

Toilets

Toilets are to be installed once the bathroom floor is finished. It is not recommended to install a toilet to the sub-floor. Affixed to the sub-floor is a 4-inch drain. From this drain, there is a plastic or metal flange, which the toilet fits over. Prior to installing the toilet, a wax seal is placed around the base of the flange. The weight of the toilet and some exerted pressure by the installer will spread and flatten the wax in such a way that it will create a leak-proof seal.

Toilets used to be flushed with as much as 5 or 7 gallons of water per flush. In older homes, tanks stood high on the wall above the toilet, and the large amount of water coupled with the height of the tank created a powerful flush. But over the years has been both an energy and natural-resource crisis, which led to a nationally mandated standard of 1.6 gallons of water per flush. Because of this new standard, most toilets in older homes will have to be updated to more modern counterparts. The following are descriptions of the different types of toilets:

- **Gravity toilets** — These 1.6-gallon, low-flow toilets are gravity-based. They come in a variety of styles and prices, and all work the same way. As the handle is pressed, a flush valve opens up, causing the water in the tank to drain into the rim openings of the bowl. Water may also pass through the large siphon-jet opening located at the bottom of the bowl, or both instances may occur.

- **Power-assist toilets** — These use a strong blast of air to push through the waste and water. Some use air compressors, but most use a pressure tank and water. Both use water forced into the air-filled pressure tank at approximately 60 psi. Due to air compression, a powerful force impacts the tank water. Once the flush button is pressed, water surges into the bowl. Because water is enclosed in a pressure tank and the pressure tank is encased inside the china toilet tank, condensation and sweating is decreased. Additionally, the immense air force of the flush creates more noise.

- **Pressure-assist toilets** — These are good for basements. They use 50 pounds of street water pressure to push waste out.

- **Vacuum-assist toilets** — Inside these toilets are two plastic tanks that together hold 1.6 gallons of water. The sole use of rim holes in the upper toilet bowl enables a clean flush. With the absence of a siphon-jet hole, all the water seeps out of the rim holes, and this allows the bowl to remain much cleaner.

- **Dual-flush toilets** — These have two buttons and use less water. There is one button for liquid wastes and another one for flushing solid wastes.

Today's toilets offer different amenities, too. There are shower toilets complete with a warm-water shower head equipped to shower the users nether regions followed by a burst of warmed air. Some have air purifiers, warmed seats, and a fan. There are specialized toilets that flush only when the lid is closed, and those that are shaped to fit in corners and other odd places.

Toilets also come in different heights. There is the standard-height model, which stands 14 inches off the ground, and then there are higher-profile toilets, which are a few inches higher. Tall people and the elderly appreciate this extra height. The standard toilet has a round bowl and extends 28 inches from the wall. Another option is the elongated, oval-shaped bowl, which extends 31 inches from the wall.

Before picking which shape to buy, measure the spot the toilet will reside on. This will determine if there is room for the elongated bowl. The cost of moving the plumbing is costly, so make sure the bowl picked will fit properly. Toilets come in a two-piece model, which is less expensive, or a one-piece model, which is manufactured as one unit.

Sinks

There are three basic types of bathroom sinks: the pedestal sink, one set into a cabinet, and the one hung on a wall. The pedestal sink is a freestanding bowl resting on a pedestal. It was a popular style found in many older homes and one that is still appreciated. However, there was a time that they fell from grace and were replaced with the vanity-style cabinet sink. This is a sink housed on top of a vanity cabinet. This style is still popular and offered in many finishes and styles.

There are cabinets made of solid wood and others made of composite materials. Solid wood is more expensive. They can accommodate single or double bowls, and the counters come in various materials like granite or marble. Bowls can drop right into a hole on the vanity, or there are bowls and counters made into one piece. A wall-hung sink is the third option but should not be used when the wall might be weak and not able to handle the weight of the bowl. They are desirable in a small room because they free up the floor space that a cabinet would occupy.

Sink bowls are typically made of vitreous china, acrylic, stone, Corian, or stainless steel. To save, it is ideal to keep the old plumbing. If it is in too bad of shape, then try and replace it, but still keep it in its original location. And if a total bathroom rehab is desired versus replacing old fixtures with new, then the re-plumbing of

A general rule of thumb is to expect that any new bathroom fixtures will not fit in the space where the old one situated. Make sure to measure the space before removing the old fixture, then measure the empty space to see if there is much wiggle room for the new fixture.

the room is likely the course that will be taken. No matter what course is taken, make sure to check with local and regional building codes to see if a licensed plumber is required to complete the work.

Restoring, Salvaging, and Replacing Older Tiles in a Home

Restoring older tiles

Many older and historic homes have fine examples of ceramic tiles that are worth keeping. Tiles are common in the kitchen, bathroom, and around the fireplace opening. Wherever they are located, it is worth the effort to save these historic gems through restoration.

The following are the steps to take for restoring older tiles:

1. If a tile has mortar on the back and side, it can be removed by placing it glazed-side down on a clean, flat and sturdy workbench. These are fragile, so properly anchor the tile, but do not put undue pressure on it. Make sure the glazed side is placed on a soft surface to prevent scratching this surface. Once secured, use a cold chisel and hammer to remove the mortar. If this method does not work, use a caustic soda, like sodium hydroxide, to soften the mortar, then use the chisel and hammer.

2. To clean the glazed surface of a tile, use warm, soapy water or bleach for ingrained stains. Many older tiles will have crazing lines. These are the fine lines and cracks that look like spider veins. They are caused over time as a house moves and settles. The stress of movement cracks the translucent finish on the top of the tile.

   Crazing can also happen when the tile is manufactured as a result of poor firing techniques or the expansion and contraction of the tile from temperature fluctuations. Over time, these crazing lines trap dirt. Some look at this result of aging as a glorious feature, but others look at it as an unsightly imperfection to be repaired. This is a personal choice. A bleach treatment may help to remove this dirt. If tiles have been used as a fireplace surround and have the soil that comes along with it, they can be cleaned with paint thinner and fine steel-wool pads.

3. Broken tiles can be glued together with clear, fast-setting acrylic glue. Assemble the pieces, glazed-side down, on a piece of newspaper. Work on a flat surface and make sure the pieces are tight and square. Apply the glue, sparingly. Prior to the glue's completely drying, clean off the excess glue with a craft knife.

Salvaging and Replacing Older Tiles

Salvaging older tiles

If all or some of the tiles in the house are beyond repair, then another option is to replace period tiles with other original tiles salvaged from a building being renovated or demolished. These are tough to find, but it might be worth networking with contractors and letting them know what you are looking for. Another resource is to purchase 18th- and 19th-century tiles from a dealer who specializes in these architectural elements.

Replacing older tiles

Replacing broken tiles can be seen as a challenge or a creative endeavor. It is difficult to replace an exact duplicate of a tile on the wall or floor. This is true for a tile installed one year ago or 100 years ago. Tiles are made in batches and even when purchasing new tiles, it is important to purchase tiles from the same batch. This is why it is critical to always purchase extra tiles. There are custom tile makers who can try to match the color and crazing effect, but this is not always 100 percent accurate. Alternatively, try removing several tiles and replacing them with a decorative tile that offers a fresh look. If some of the tiles are broken around the edges of a floor or wall, remove all of the edge tiles and put down all new tiles in a different color or pattern to create a new eye-catching border. Another approach to take with replacing older tiles on a wall is to replace an entire wall instead of just replacing a few. An entire wall will complement an adjacent wall, unlike what would occur with installing replacement tiles that are an inaccurate match. Finally, another option is to purchase reproductions of historic and classic tiles.

CASE STUDY: SUBWAY TILE REPRODUCTION COMPANY

Keith Bieneman
Subway Ceramics
303 Bruce Street
Verona, Wisconsin 53593
888-387-3280
www.SubwayCeramics.com

The style of ceramic tile known as the "subway" tile was first manufactured during the Victorian era in the late 1800s. This was the only type of tile being manufactured in the United States, and the mass production of them lasted until the middle of the 1940s. After WWII, the styles and colors produced began to change. This was in part due to more advanced manufacturing techniques; plus, consumers decorated their homes with tiles in different styles and colors and moved away from the flat, white tiles with the thin grout lines.

Consumers continued to appreciate the classic subway-tile style for more than 100 years. These tiles were notably used in the subways of New York City and other transit systems around the United States, and this is how they got their name. Recently, New York City has made an effort to painstakingly restore these flat tiles from the early 1900s. Many homes built between the 1890s through the 1940s still have original black-and-white subway tiles on bathroom and kitchen walls and floors. Some even have these tiles adorning the fireplace surround. Today, many homeowners of older and historic homes are committed to refurbishing or replacing their subway tiles.

Manufacturers in various parts of the world mass produce tiles that have a similar look to the subway tile; they can be purchased at home improvement stores and tile retailers. However, if a homeowner is in terested in finding a more realistic and authentic reproduction of the subway tile, which is not mass-produced, then consider using those manufactured by Subway Ceramics. This is a specialty ceramic tile company with their corporate headquarters in Verona, Wisconsin, and their manufacturing plant in southern California.

They exclusively produce a full line of subway tiles and complementing accessories to be used in older, historic, or new homes. By the 1920s, tile manufacturers conformed to making the same uniform sizes for their wall and mosaic floor tiles. "This makes it simpler for Subway Ceramics to make a collection of tiles that will be able to fit and replace the subway tiles found in most homes," said company owner Keith Bieneman.

Six years ago, Bieneman started Subway Ceramics to fill a void in tile offerings. "I saw the annual introduction of new and different tile products, but there was not a manufacturer producing a traditional product like the subway tile. I interacted with many homeowners who wanted a more traditional tile to install in their old home to restore it back to its original character," Bieneman said.

As the company name implies, Bieneman recreates various subway tiles, trims, and moldings, ranging from simple to elegant designs. "What makes this company different is it makes the effort to create a historically authentic architectural building material that one would find in period homes beginning during the turn of the century," Bieneman said. To avoid the appearance of mass production, all tiles are created in the United States in smaller amounts.

Homeowners who are passionate about trying to replace all the elements in their older homes with original or exact replicas of existing materials know that finding building materials can be a daunting challenge. Preserving the original character of a home can be time-consuming and costly. Owners who have the desire to learn about ways to put things back to the way they were originally built are continually faced with making choices.

"These homeowners see themselves as the stewards of their older homes and want to keep the original character," Bieneman said. "Although my tiles might be more expensive than mass-produced ones, they are historically authentic, still affordable, and maintain the distinctive character of a room — and are a practical alternative."

The most common sizes of subway tiles available from Subway Ceramics are the following:

- 3 by 6 inches   • 6 by 6 inches
- 2 by 6 inches   • 4.25 by 4.25 inches

Tiles come in the traditional-gloss white and black colors, as well as other period colors. They also make tiles with a crackle-glaze finish. "The crackle-glaze finish is created to reproduce the effect that occurs when crazing lines form in a translucent glaze and are reflected by the ambient light penetrating the glaze layer. This is a decorative effect that is produced in a somewhat controlled manner by creating stress between the glaze and the tile bisque," Bieneman said.

The stress is achieved by formulating the glaze with a coefficient of expansion slightly different from that of the bisque. As the tile cools following the glaze-firing stage, this mismatch in the coefficient of expansion forms a uniform network of random crackle features. Several original subway tiles placed on today's walls contain lines due to house movement. These lines will keep forming on the surfaces of the tiles, more visible in some areas as opposed to others.

"This can clearly be seen in vintage installations where translucent glazes were used as decorative liners. Solid, opaque white wall tiles will also form crazing lines gradually, and these features are revealed when stained over the course of time," Bieneman said. The natural impact of tile aging is visible in vintage installations and adds unique character to the surfaces of the tiles. "Solid-color glazes are less likely to show crazing lines even when stained. Their glaze lacks the depth and luster of a classic translucent glaze," he said.

Today, Subway Ceramics tiles are used for renovating older homes but also used in newly constructed homes. The company's mission is to educate consumers on how to best preserve the original character of their kitchens and bathrooms. They continue to revive this uniquely American craft because consumers continue to appreciate the design style.

"It is best if the homeowner uses a tile-installing professional on projects, and he should be experienced in restoration work. This is encouraged because many will use the older tile-installation techniques versus the more modern methods used today. Plus, installers help with ordering the right amount of product and will stand behind their work," Bieneman said.

Homeowners can only purchase Subway Ceramics through specialty-tile retailers of trade professionals because of the technical and historic nature of their tiles. For more information about the products, or to get started on a restoration project, visit Subway Ceramics' Web site at **www.subwayceramics.com**.

CHAPTER 12

Extra Rooms and Details

Basements

Remodeling a basement adds a tremendous living space and opens the house to an increased amount of activity and entertainment. Renovating a basement is an immediate addition to the square footage of usable space in a house and will increase its real estate value.

To transform the basement, assess what is there now and what can be changed. For instance, the heating system, electrical system, hot water tank, and plumbing pipes might be in the basement. To save on costs, these important systems need to remain where they are, but can be camouflaged. The location of the plumbing will be important if a bathroom or wet bar is part of the renovation design.

Take care of any open, bare piping and ducts that may be obvious on the ceiling. They can be hidden and protected. If additional plumbing is needed, it may need to be installed under the flooring. Basement flooring is usually made of concrete, so be prepared to do some manual labor. Consider having pipes rest above the floor. The floor and walls may need to have the cracks filled in, and additional walls, partitions, and doors may need to be added.

The next task on the list is to check out the electrical system of the basement. Any electrical appliances for the remodeled basement must have the appropriate voltage, so additional outlets and circuits might be needed. Figure out where they are needed during the planning phase because placing an electrical outlet in the wrong place will cause more unwanted expenses and delays. Acoustic tiles are a smart move for the ceiling of the basement because they give easy access to the plumbing and utilities for the rest of the house.

Consider the ventilation and humidity conditions in the basement. If it is musty, then what is causing this musty smell? Is there a lack of ventilation? If there is a crawl space, is the soil moldy? Is moisture an ongoing problem in the basement? Before renovating the basement, take care of any ventilation or moisture problems. If the basement takes on water after it rains, then look into installing a sump pump to protect the flooring and furnishings in the newly renovated room.

Is there an adequate presence of natural light? If not, what type of lighting will be installed to compensate for few or no windows? One of the last steps to a basement remodel is to make changes and repairs to the floor of the basement. These changes will be impacted by whether the sub-floor is made of concrete or wood.

If it is made of concrete, then ceramic tiles are a nice choice. If the concrete floor is in good condition, then covering the floor with paint made specifically for concrete is an option, rather than accenting with area rugs. Another option is to add a new skim coat of concrete over the existing floor and stain the new layer. If there is a wooden sub-floor with damage to it, then repair damages and choose a floor covering that accommodates the main activity of the room.

Attics

Attics are often the one space in a home underutilized. Depending on its configuration, an attic could be the ideal space for a family room, extra bedrooms, a home office, or a home theater. The ceiling, however, must be at least 7½ feet in height in order to convert an attic space into functional living space other than storage. An attic can also be a foundation to build another floor onto the home. The following are key points to consider when expanding the attic in an older home:

- Are there stairs, or is there a pull down ladder to access the attic? If there are no stairs, is the cost of building a set of stairs feasible, practical, or cost-prohibitive? If there are stairs that lead to the attic, are they safe? Is the staircase wide enough and built at the right pitch to allow use on a daily basis? If you want to install an attic ladder, do you know where to install it?

- How will you get the building materials into the attic?

- Is there electricity to the attic? If no, how will it be brought there? If yes, is it adequate and safe?

- Do you know how to divert electricity or air ducts?

- Are there building codes and permits required to renovate the attic?

- Is the space insulated to protect the house from the heat and cold? Is the insulation helping to conserve fuel costs by keeping the heat inside during the winter and the cool air inside in the summer?

- Is it properly ventilated with windows, vents, fans, or louvers?

- Is there enough natural light, or are windows, dormers, or skylights needed? Is it possible to install them?

- If there is a chimney in the attic, is it in good condition? Does it have water stains or creosote streaks on it? If there is creosote, it is worth having the chimney cleaned to make sure the flue liner to the chimney is working properly.

- The ceiling joists need to be well built to carry the extra live and dead loads potentially created when an attic is converted to living space. Live loads are designated as foot traffic, and dead loads are the furniture and other items including storage. Joists must be 12 inches or more in thickness to be considered sturdy enough to handle the load.

Attics need to be protected from water entering the home from the roof, vents, and chimneys. Preventing these kinds of leaks and water damage will protect the floor of the attic and any floors below. Attics need proper ventilation to limit moisture problems created by water vapor and condensation. Attics need to be insulated to limit the loss of heat or air conditioning from the lower floors.

The design and construction of the roof will either hinder or help when creating living spaces in an attic. Rafter and truss systems are the most common roof systems. Ridge beams, in which rafter roof attics are centered, extend down the roof system center at the highest section. To finish the roof, additional lumber links to the ridge beam and plywood are placed on the frame. They are put together piece by piece and are usually made from a 2x6 instead of a 2x4.

The truss roof is faster to put up than a rafter system. They are normally 2x4 and made of yellow pine. As opposed to the rafter type roof composed of pieces of lumber, truss systems are created in workshops and are prepared for installation upon arrival. According to experts, the most common, traditional rafters are able to last as long as a truss system.

Once installation is complete, truss roofs cannot be altered. This is due to the design of trusses, made to use less wood and bear more weight. By altering the truss and cutting parts off, its capacity to carry weight changes. Rafter systems are more spacious and well suited for attics. If your attic already has trusses, they cannot be changed, and you will need to find a way to work in their presence.

Often, people get so excited by the thought of the new living space that they forget about the basics. Have a game plan in place before you start the project. Create a drawing prior to starting. This will help you with the floor layout, and what materials and tradespeople you will need to complete the project. This also will enable you to create a budget so you will have an understanding of the amount of money you will need for the project.

Individual and Shared Rooms

Family rooms, dens, and other areas where families congregate may be in need of renovation or creation. Older homes were not built with the activities and needs of today's family in mind. However, there may be an extra room or area that can be converted into a shared room. An extra bedroom, attic, or basement might serve as a room to be converted into a library, den, or hobby room for family recreational activities.

Home office

Is there a need for a home office? Does someone have a business that requires an office, or could it be used for the family members to use the computer? Determine what activities are going to take place in this room, and plan for some or all of the following elements in the home office:

- A desk area
- Storage
- Shelving

- Bookcases
- Filing cabinets
- Computer equipment
- A meeting table
- Couch or easy chairs

Home theaters

Another popular trend is to create a room filled with various types of electronic media. This has become a place for families to spend time together watching movies and playing electronic games. Older homes will not have made allowances for this type of room or the electrical needs, but a room can be re-wired to accommodate all of the various types of equipment desired.

Porches

The porch serves as both a design feature and a functional structure for the house. It protects the entryways and people from the sun, wind, rain, snow, and cold. The entryway to a house can offer an inviting and friendly welcome to visitors. The porch, if properly situated and symmetric in relation to the shape of the house, can enhance the physical attractiveness of the home.

Porches can be screened-in or glassed-in to offer additional living, relaxing, and working spaces for the occupants. It is often seen as a transitional area between the outdoor and indoor spaces. Sometimes it is best to remove a porch when it is poorly placed and makes the appearance of the home look awkward. At other times, it is best to add a porch or stoop to complement the entrance.

Adding this extra living space to a home increases its value as well as its appeal. The porch is an entrance to a home supported by columns with a roof covering that does not cover a wall. The piazza is a large, covered porch that covers a wall. The stoop is a small platform with a roof that may or may not have steps.

The architectural design of the home can dictate if the porch has been properly designed and well suited to the overall appearance of the home. If building a porch, make sure to take into consideration the architectural character of the home and see that the porch complements this style. An evaluation is necessary to determine the best course of action for the porch: repair, demolish, or replace.

The porch is a common place where home repairs are necessary due to its daily exposure to the elements. If a porch already exists, then it might suffer from damaged and decayed wood caused by water or attacks by insects. If porches are not properly painted and sealed, the damages can quickly escalate. Regular maintenance and simple repairs using paint, caulk, and moldings can keep a porch in good condition. There are typical repairs needed to make porches safe and functioning properly. The following are the most common areas and problems to check on a porch to determine its condition:

- The stairs of a porch are typically made of wood, concrete, or other masonry products, such as brick. Over time, wood can decay, and masonry products can crack, break, or become loosened and will need repair or replacement. If stairs are directly on the ground, they become subject to frosts and heaves from freezing temperatures, which can alter their shape and soundness.

- The floor and floorboards of the porch can decay due to weather, water, insect attacks, and foundation problems, and they may need repair or replacement. Sometimes only a few floorboards will need to be replaced to correct the problem.

- The roof of a porch needs to be securely affixed to the house. Check supports and braces to make sure they have a strong connection to the house.

- The ceiling of a porch roof can be affected if the roof of the porch is not properly supported or if there are foundation problems.

- The railings can become loose from decay and use and will create a safety issue.

- The bottom of columns, supports, or posts, especially if they are made of wood, are susceptible to decay from exposure to moisture.

- The foundation of a porch needs to be able to hold the weight of the elements of the porch, such as the roof and the columns. Check to see if the foundation is in good condition to support the porch and keep it level.

- Joints are susceptible to water damage and decay if not properly sealed and maintained.

Termites can decrease the life of any porch made with wood. When building an outside structure such as a porch, avoid allowing wood to have any direct contact with the ground to minimize termite infestation. When building or replacing wood members, use pressure-treated lumber that is kiln-dried after treatment (KDAT) to help a porch last longer.

There are also woods that are naturally resistant to termites, like turpentine trees, white cypress, and any of the sequoias. Even these naturally resistant trees can fall victim to an infestation if it is large enough. Untreated lumber can be kept off the ground by using termite-resistant concrete, steel, or masonry foundations. Termites are still capable of damaging some of these termite-resistant barriers and have been known to chew through soft plastics and even harder substances like lead to get to the moist wood; therefore, it is recommended to still use treated lumber. For best results, new structures should be built with implanted physical termite barriers that considerably halt their entrance.

Sunrooms

The precursor to the sunroom was the Victorian English conservatory for the purpose of providing an indoor garden during the winter months. Today's sunroom is less elaborate but still offers a sunny spot to grow plants and enjoy the warmth of the sun on a cold day. When designing a new sunroom, make sure it is facing an exposure that will provide a lot of sun.

Also, design the room so it will complement the style of the house. The room will need lots of windows, so select them carefully. Choose large enough windows so the room will get a large amount of sun, and make sure condensation will not be a problem. Have some solid walls — not all windows — so the room will not get too hot. Ceramic and quarry-tile floors complement the room.

Use a darker color for the walls, because a white-walled sunroom can be blinding. Also, white paint deteriorates quicker than darker color paint when exposed to greater-than-normal amounts of sunlight. Furnishing a sunroom can be fun by using wrought iron, wicker, or rattan items that can be moved out to a patio or deck in the warmer weather.

If a sunroom already exists, then the biggest repairs will be with windows. These rooms in an older or historic home will have energy-inefficient windows, so the decision will be whether to replace them or find a storm window suitable to match the house and still offer the sunny ambiance of the room. *See "An Alternative Window for Energy Efficiency" in Chapter 9.*

The Details

Patios and decks are outdoor rooms with a view to the landscape of a home. Swimming pools and spas are places to exercise, play, and unwind. They are all parts of the home to relax, entertain, grow plants, and daydream. Decks and patios will be built on the ground and attached to the house, or in close proximity to it.

These outdoor features will enhance the enjoyment residents get from their home. If a patio or deck does not exist, then decide if adding one is feasible. If one or both are already in existence, then evaluate the condition to determine if they are in satisfactory shape. They may require some minor renovations; if the condition is poor, then decide if major renovations, demolition, or replacement is required. Swimming pools and decks are water features that offer families hours of fun and relaxation, and can increase the value of a home, as long as they are functioning and properly placed.

Patio and deck designs

Patios and decks can be made of many different materials and can take the shape of numerous configurations. Patios and decks must be attached to the house or in close proximity to it. In many instances, it is an extension of the indoor living spaces. For instance, a patio or deck might be built off a living room, dining room, or kitchen. This provides easy access to the kitchen, bathroom, and other interior activities.

The design also needs to provide a smooth transition between indoor and outdoor spaces. The design, size, and construction of a patio or deck will depend on the layout of the house, the location, the lifestyle of the occupants, and its intended use. The weather is another component that affects the design. Features and furnishings will be adapted according to the amount of rain, snow, sun, or wind an area receives. Is the space primarily for use in the warm weather, colder weather, or both?

This will determine if a roof and wall structures need to be incorporated in the design. If the house is located in the South, then adding a roof to shelter people from the heat of the day is important. The same holds true if the house is located in the Pacific Northwest where there are many rainy days. If it is in the Northeast, then the patio will probably not be used in the winter, but if it has a roof, it will need to be sturdy to handle the weight of the snow.

Patio construction

The first phase of constructing a patio begins with selecting the proper site and designing a plan. The design can be simple or complex. This is up to the individual, the budget, and the location. Patios, at a minimum, need a floor. The other parts of patio are walls and overhead protectors; these features are optional.

The design possibilities are endless once the flooring material has been selected. Wood, screens, fencing, lattice, planters, solid walls, canvas, glass, plastic, and fiberglass panels can be added to create the outdoor space. The space and desired look will dictate the addition of these materials and features.

The patio space should at least be able to accommodate the number of people who live in the home, then add space to make allowances for entertaining. To figure out the measurement, remember that for one person to be comfortable with one chair, she will require at least 20 square feet; therefore, to accommodate 20 people, the patio needs to be 400 square feet.

A patio must be constructed on a fairly flat and permeable ground surface. The slope should be no more than 6 degrees. The ground should be made of a mix of sand, rock, and silt. This will make the most stable foundation for the patio. The following are the materials usually used for patios:

- **Bricks** — These come in a variety of colors and designs, and can be arranged in intricate and unique patterns, many with different colors. Bricks can heave with a frost, so they might be impractical in colder climates.

- **Patio pavers** — These are made of concrete and come in different shapes and colors. They are manufactured specifically for patios, so the design potential is endless.

- **Stone** — This comes from a stone that has been cut flat on both sides. Natural stone like flagstone is a popular and highly desirable patio flooring material. Flagstone can be either formal or informal, depending on how it is laid out. The flagstone is installed in a patio similar to how ceramic tiles are laid on a kitchen floor. They are set in the ground in a layer of mortar. Over time, the mortar will fall out and loosen. To restore it, use a mixture of sand and pre-mixed mortar mix. Adding sand to the pre-mixed mortar mix helps it to blend with the older mortar.

- **Concrete** — The use of concrete offers a variety of design possibilities. Concrete, however, does crack in colder climates. One solution to this problem is to use wood strips as expansion joints. Concrete comes in a variety of colors, and the methods used to treat the surface create an interesting flooring option.

Deck construction

The deck is a horizontal structure that is built on the ground and is mostly made of wood. Unlike a patio, a deck can be raised above the ground by inches or feet and might have a stairway attached. Also, a deck can be built below ground level (depending on the location and design of the home), or where there is sloped or poorly graded land. This works well because of the inherent design feature of having an adjustable support system. The beauty and flexibility of a deck is in the fact that it can be designed to accommodate all heights and grade levels of ground and homes.

Wooden decks do not complement all styles of homes, so make sure they are suitable for the overall look of the home. Decks can be built at floor level or as an extension off a higher story in the house. They can also have multiple levels to make a separate place for cooking, dining, or as a private location for a hot tub.

Decks are more casual than a patio because they are built out of wood but still allow for a relaxed and entertaining surrounding. Roofs and walls are optional features with decks, but a simple trellis can serve as a wall for vines to grow. If the deck is built more than a few feet off the ground, it should have a railing feature for safety. Many decks have built-in benches that function as both seating and safety.

Renovating a deck

As with a patio, if the home already has a deck, evaluate its condition. Be sure it is safe and sturdy enough to accommodate a number of guests at one time. Check the condition of the wood for decay from insects or water damage, and check the fasteners to make sure they are secure.

Minor repairs will include replacing, re-staining or re-painting the wood, or building a new railing. If the condition is beyond repair, consider rebuilding it. Many decks have been made of cedar or pretreated wood so they will last longer. If rebuilding, repairing, or building a deck for the first time, note that there are more material options today. In addition, there are deck-building products and systems that are now made out of non-wood materials that will not rot or be affected by insect damage.

Pools and spas

Swimming pools are a feature, which seem to be either highly desirable or not wanted at all. In certain parts of the country, swimming pools are in great demand and add to the value of a home, but in other regions they are optional and not as significant. If the home already has a pool, then decide if you want to keep it.

This decision might be based on condition and lifestyle. If you want to keep it, then determine if it needs repairs or is in good working order. If the home does not have a pool and you want one, then factor in the following considerations when making a decision on location and design:

- Pool choice — whether an in-ground pool or above-ground pool is best based on location and landforms

- Costs to build and maintain the pool

- Local and regional building codes

- Insurance liabilities and requirements

- Legal issues and requirements involving power and utility lines, easements, and where the water will drain out

- Logistical issues concerning the property, landscape, land, and soil

- Social constraints in a neighborhood

- Building other structures, like a cabana to change clothes, a spa, fences, decks, surrounds, walls, greenhouses, and gazebos

Spas include at least a whirlpool tub or hot tub, which allow the user to sit and soak in approximately 4 feet of warm water. The relaxation and health benefits of a spa make them a great place to unwind at the end of the day or invite guests to enjoy. They may be built in close proximity to a swimming pool, and then they can share a common filtration system and heating unit.

A wet/dry sauna may also be included in the spa. A deck is an ideal location to build a spa if one already exists. Other locations are suitable; the final choice depends on the layout of the property, the weather, and the best spot to take advantage of a good view and have some privacy. If the house already has a spa feature, then determine the condition and decide if you want to keep them. If the house does not have a spa and you want one, then figure out where it should be located and what you want to include in the spa.

The landscaping

The rules for landscaping property can be simple or elaborate. The work can be done while interior renovations are taking place, or in stages over several years. Actually, it is better to wait and live in the home and learn about how the weather impacts the property and what activities the residents want to do outdoors.

Some homeowners enjoy this part of owning a home and consider it a labor of love; others consider it a distraction from their real passions. Prior to investing in new lawns, shrubs, trees, and other plant materials, consider how other work on the property will impact any landscaping efforts. Planning a sequence of renovating events will prevent damage to plantings and exterior structures. Here are other points to consider:

- Will you design the space, plant the materials, and maintain the outside setting?
- Will a landscaper be hired to do all or part of the work?
- Will the plantings be in the way if the exterior of the house is painted?
- Will heavy equipment vehicles run over the new lawn?

- Will the staging and old roofing materials damage shrubs around the foundation?

The outside of the home is meant to be a place of relaxation, function, and recreation. Plan and plant according to the site, the surroundings, the climate, and the individual needs of the residents. Design according to budget, maintenance requirements, and taste. If you do not want to spend much time mowing a lawn and caring for plants, then design the space accordingly.

If you love an herb, flower, and vegetable garden and do not mind the labor involved, then make space to include these features in your outside area. If there is a deck, pool, or patio, make sure to incorporate these structures into the landscape plan. Are there walkways, paths, walls, steps, fences, ponds, and other features that bring people to the various places on the property? Do these features already exist, or will they be built or installed? If they already exist, are they in good condition? If not, decide if they will remain, be moved, replaced, or repaired.

Trees offer an attractive and functional purpose. They can offer shade to help save on air conditioning bills and comfort to those sitting under them on a hot day. They can help to lessen the impact of wind blowing directly on the house, which saves on the heating bill.

Remember to pick the best trees for the locations where they are going to be placed. Be sure not to plant trees too closely to the house, the driveway, the septic system, power lines, or any other structure that can be damaged by roots, sap, leaves or falling branches. If the label on a 6-foot tall tree states it will grow to 40 feet, then it probably will.

Landscaping materials can be purchased from local nurseries, home improvement stores, and catalogs. Buying local usually guarantees that these plant materials will be hardy and thrive in the climate they were purchased from.

If buying from a catalog company located in a warmer climate, make sure the plant materials are suitable for winter climates; similarly, when buying plants in a colder climate, make sure they can grow in a warmer climate. For instance, birch trees do better in colder climates of New England than they do in the warmer regions of the country.

A landscaping game plan

There are many details to think about when planning or refurbishing outside spaces. It also depends on the expertise of the do-it-yourselfer. If working outside is a passion, then this part of renovating will be a joy. It might be a good idea to get some design help if required. But if working in the yard is not something one looks forward to, then it is best to consider getting some help for both the design and the actual labor part of the job.

There are different types of professionals one can hire to help with outdoor spaces. They will have different training backgrounds, education, qualifications, and capabilities. Hiring one type of professional may be sufficient, or it may be necessary to hire a combination of skilled individuals or companies, depending on the scope and scale of the project. Here is a brief description of each professional in the landscaping arena:

- **Landscape architects** — These are licensed professionals with at least four years of education in the field. Landscape architects have studied horticulture, engineering, geology, meteorology, biology, and art history. The American Society of Landscape Architects (ASLA) usually accredits schools offering degrees in landscape architecture. Landscape architects must graduate from a school accredited by the ASLA and obtain a license.

  State licenses mean there is a legal requirement and responsibility attached to them. They offer services in landscape design, site planning, feasibility studies, and landscape design solutions and alternatives. They can draw general or specific plans for the landscape and can assist with land countouring, walkways, driveways, swimming pools, decks, courtyards, sewage lines, outdoor structures, and plant materials.

- **Landscape designers** — These are professionals involved in many of the same projects a landscape architect might work on, but they do not hold a license; therefore, there are no legal requirements affiliated with this title. Primary responsibilities include selecting plant materials, locating them throughout the outdoor spaces, and planning for the construction and installation features like pavements, outdoor lighting, retaining walls, pathways, steps, and other yard features. They study horticulture, and many of the larger nurseries have a few designers on their staff. Commonly, either a client or a landscape contractor will hire the designer to provide the aesthetically pleasing plan for the space.

- **Landscape contractors** — These are the professionals who will execute the design plan. They are independent business owners and have their own work crew. Often, they hire the landscape architect or designer on an as-needed basis to design a space. They work to place and plant materials, and to construct features.

- **Nursery workers** — These professionals grow and sell the plant materials. They can also incorporate landscape architecture and design in their business in order to offer a full range of services to their clientele.

- **Gardeners** — They may or may not have an education related to their work, but usually have lots of experience with choosing, planting, nurturing, and maintaining gardens for their clients.

Review Chapter 1 for general tips on hiring. Always get some form of a contract so it is clearly spelled out who will do what tasks, when, and for how much. Below are the key points to remember when hiring and for the terms of the contract:

- Get three bids from reputable professionals on any larger projects.

- Read contracts over carefully and understand what they mean before signing.

- Make sure all tasks to be completed are thoroughly described.

- Find out when the work will be completed.

- Find out any extra charges to be added to the invoice.

- Get an itemized list of all plants and materials to be used, and their costs.

- See who will get permits and arrange for inspections, if required.

- Ask if the companies are insured, bonded, have general liability coverage, and workers' compensation for their employees.

- Find out if the professional is responsible for any damages done as a result of the work.

- See who is responsible for hauling away debris.

- Find out what the responsibilities and liabilities are for each party.

- Ask what the method of payment is and when it is expected.

- If subcontractors are to be hired, ask who will supervise and pay them. Are they insured and bonded?

- Get and check references.

- See completed projects similar to your design.

Outdoor spaces can be designed and decorated to match the personal taste of the homeowner. They can be formal, informal, rustic, and whimsical. They can include all or some of the following activities and features:

- Incorporate hammocks, lounge chairs, and seating areas to relax.

- Make room for a sand box, swing set, and maybe a tree house. Children and adults will like having a space to play badminton, croquet, horseshoes, football, baseball, volleyball, and soccer. For adults, consider a hot tub or spa.

- Meet any needs for seating, eating, standing areas, and barbecue/ cooking facilities.

- Make use of trees, shrubs, annuals, perennials, ornamental grasses, succulents, tropical plants, and roses to decorate the outdoor space.

- Grow herbs and vegetables in an outdoor space to serve as a functional and attractive garden.

- Feed the birds (and other wildlife) with birdfeeders and birdbaths.

- Create water features such as fountains, water gardens, waterfalls, and ponds.

- Use window boxes, planters, urns, tubs, baskets, troughs, and trellises to grow colorful plants and flowers.

- Complement the house and yard with shade structures that offer a place to get out of the sun and grow plant materials. There are several to choose from that have a roof and may or may not have solid walls. Options include structures like gazebos, porticos, atriums, pergolas, arbors, trellises, and pavilions.

- Outdoor furniture might be needed for different spaces such as dining areas, sun bathing, and sitting areas with benches, chairs, and side tables.

Fireplaces and wood stoves

Many looking to buy a home have a fireplace or a wood stove on their "want list." From a design perspective, they offer a decorating focal point that Realtors use as a selling point. On a more practical side, the heat output can help reduce heating costs.

When purchasing or living in an older home, it is important to make certain the fireplace, wood stove, and chimney are not a fire hazard. Have a professional conduct an inspection to offer an evaluation of the heating units and to ascertain if any repairs or renovations are required. Building codes will dictate some of the requirements of fireplaces and wood stoves.

Many repairs will require special skills, so it is best to leave them to the professionals. There are some renovations, such as brick or stone repair and repainting that homeowners can do. Improving the look of the fireplace surround, mantel, or the appearance of a wood stove should be done after the safety check is completed.

Fireplaces can use wood as fuel or can be fitted with gas logs to alleviate the work and mess. There are also heat inserts that can be installed inside the opening of the fireplace. This is a heating unit that fits into the opening of the fireplace and has a built-in fan. When a fire is burning, the unit has the ability to take in cold air and blow out hot air. There is a glass door to open and close to build and tend to the fire, as well as to enjoy the flickering of the flames.

Fireplaces are not the most efficient way to produce heat, and most of the heat goes up the chimney. But with an insert, the fans blow the heat into the room, and a homeowner can save on her heating bills. Insert costs can begin at approximately $1,000 but will pay for themselves in a few heating seasons with savings on the heating bill.

From a design standpoint, a fireplace should fit the style of the house. An old-fashioned, carved-wood mantel will look out of place in a contemporary home, just as an ornate marble mantel and fireplace surround will look out of scale in a small, 1920s bungalow. The size of the fireplace should fit the size and scale of the house.

If the mantel and fireplace is too big or too small, it will look out of proportion to the rest of the room. If there are fireplaces in several rooms of a historic home and you choose not to use them, they can be closed off. The mantel can remain for decorative and historic purposes.

It is important to keep chimneys, fireplaces, and wood stoves in safe, working order. Local and regional building codes will dictate the chimney design to promote safety. The following are the key questions to ask in relation to these heating units and their operation:

- Is there a damper?
- Is the outer hearth at least 16 inches in the front of a firebox and far enough away, on either side, from the chimney box?
- Do the fireplace, wood stove, and chimney meet local building codes?
- Does the chimney have a flue?
- Is the chimney clean?
- Is the chimney in disrepair?

Chimneys

Chimneys need to be inspected both inside and out to determine their safety status and condition prior to use. Here are the key components to a chimney and the concerns a homeowner needs to address in regard to chimney safety:

- Most chimneys will be made of stone or brick with a special heat-resistant mortar. This is considered the wall of the chimney and should be made out of 4-inch-thick brick. Make sure that all the bricks or stone are in place and that the mortar is not crumbling or missing. Repairing a chimney in an older home is a reasonable project for a do-it-yourselfer to accomplish. However, if the home is historic, the project is more complex and is best left to the professionals who are experienced in chimney restoration.

- Chimneys need a flue liner to carry smoke and sparks out into the open air. These liners can be made out of baked clay tiles (terra cotta), a rigid stainless-steel pipe, or a proprietary cementitious mix. The flue should be at least $5/8$-inch thick. Clay flue liners offer a safety feature to a chimney because they promote less creosote build up. Flues need to be clear, fireproof, and free of cracks. This can be determined by using a powerful flashlight and shining it up the flue to look for any cracks.

  Older homes may not have a flue liner in their chimney and should not be used. There is one exception to this rule: If the chimney is made with three courses of brick and heat-resistant mortar, then it is possible to use the chimney. Prior to use, have the local fire department inspect it for safety.

- Chimneys need a damper. This is a device that closes off the fireplace from the chimney. Prior to lighting a fire, make sure the damper is operable. It will usually have a few settings that allow the damper to be opened wider. The wider the damper is open, the more heat will go up the chimney. Make sure the damper is opened before lighting a fire, so that smoke goes up the chimney instead of into the house. When the fireplace is not in use, close the damper because an open damper will draw house heat up the chimney. Before starting the next fire, remember to check to see if the damper is open. This is a common step users forget to take.

- When has the chimney last been cleaned? Or has it ever been cleaned? Creosote builds up on the inside of the chimney, which can cause a fire.

- The top of the chimney needs to be at least 3 feet tall, beginning at the point it extends out of the roof. Also, the chimney must extend at least 2 feet above any point on the roof or part of the house.

CONCLUSION

After reading this book, you should realize that a lot of hard work goes into renovating an older home, and see that it is important to save money while performing routine repairs. Additionally, you must be sure to abide by all the rules set by local officials in terms of home renovation. All instances of asbestos, radon, and lead must be examined and removed by the appropriate professionals.

Having the right skills and equipment is also an essential element in renovation. When you feel unsure about a certain repair or just want some help, you can always gain assistance in home renovation through federal, state, and local programs. Historic societies are also available to aid with this process.

Whether repairing your roof, water system, or interior framework, do not get discouraged. Although this may be an intense, laborious process, you will benefit tremendously by the end results. With outside help and the right tools and resources, you will successfully renovate your home in no time. *Good luck!*

APPENDIX A

Home Inspection Evaluation Checklist

	EXCELLENT	GOOD	ACCEPTABLE	POOR	VERY POOR	COST TO REPAIR
BASEMENT						
Foundation						
Sills						
Beams						
Supporting posts						
Joists						
Sub-flooring						
Under-floors						
Furnace						
Heating pipes						
Water lines						
Sewer lines						
Electrical wiring						
Hot water heater						
Moisture						
Cracks in floor						
Insulation						
FOUNDATION						
Cracks						
Settling						
Water problems						

	EXCELLENT	GOOD	ACCEPTABLE	POOR	VERY POOR	COST TO REPAIR
Crumbling/heaving						
ROOF						
General condition						
Sags						
Rotting members						
Life expectancy of shingles						
Valleys						
Flashing						
Gutters						
Ridge line						
Dormers						
Chimney						
Tree interference						
Stains						
1st floor						
Framing sill						
Plates and joists						
PLUMBING						
Water pressure						
Life expectancy						
Leaks if water is turned on						

	EXCELLENT	GOOD	ACCEPTABLE	POOR	VERY POOR	COST TO REPAIR
ELECTRICAL						
Fuse or circuit breaker						
Electrical outlets						
Switches/receptacles						
Light fixtures						
Wiring						
Adequacy of service for now and in future						
EXTERIOR						
Siding						
Masonry						
Windows						
Window sills						
Settling						
Decoration						
Walls						
Doors						
Soffit						
Fascia boards						
Rotting						
Cracks in bricks, stone, block						

	EXCELLENT	GOOD	ACCEPTABLE	POOR	VERY POOR	COST TO REPAIR
LIVING AREAS						
Floors						
Walls						
Ceilings						
Windows						
Number of rooms						
Layout of rooms						
Bathroom						
Kitchen						
WATER & SEWER						
Well recovery						
Septic system						
Standing water						
Odors						
Water pressure						
FIREPLACE						
Chimneys						
Wood stove						
HEATING & COOLING						
Condition						
Adequacy						

	EXCELLENT	GOOD	ACCEPTABLE	POOR	VERY POOR	COST TO REPAIR
Life expectancy						
INSULATION						
Is there any?						
Condition						
APPLIANCES						
Inventory						
Condition						
Do they stay?						
PORCHES						
Design						
Decoration						
Posts						
Balusters						
Steps						
Floor						
Under						
Structure						
Roof						
HEALTH & SAFETY						
Radon						
Lead water/lead paint						

	EXCELLENT	GOOD	ACCEPTABLE	POOR	VERY POOR	COST TO REPAIR
Asbestos						
Fire safety						
Emergency exits						
Smoke detectors						
Sprinklers						
Coal/wood stoves						
Electrical wiring						
ATTIC						
Insulation						
Leaks						
Potential space for rooms						
Storage capabilities						
Wiring						
Windows						
INSECTS						
Termites						
Carpenter ants						
Powder-post beetles						
Rodents						
Snakes						

GLOSSARY

OF TERMS

A-frame — A structure where the main walls lean together to form an A-shaped roof.

Acoustical tile — Made to monitor sound volume and serve as a cover to walls or ceilings, this is a specialized tile composed of mineral, wood and cork, vegetable fibers, or metal.

Air duct — Specialized piping that transfers warm and cold air around the house and over to the furnace or air conditioning system.

Ampere — The rate used to measure the flow of electricity through electrical wires.

Anchor bolt — A specialized bolt used to secure the sill plate to the foundation walls or masonry floors.

Asbestos — A silica-based mineral found in insulation and other materials; known to cause cancer.

Asphalt — Residue from evaporated petroleum. Widely used as a waterproofing agent in the manufacture of many waterproof roof coverings, exterior wall coverings, flooring tile, etc.

Atrium — This is a partially enclosed interior courtyard room that dates back to Greek and Roman times. It is considered a room in nature where entertaining and relaxing takes place.

Attic ventilator — A mechanism used to ventilate an attic space. They are screened openings; the inlet unit will be found at the soffit area, and the outlet unit will be at the gable ends or along the ridge of the roof system. Electric fans are also used to ventilate the attic.

Backfill — The earth or gravel that is placed around a house to fill a gap after the foundation has been poured.

Backsplash — The surface area of wall directly behind the sink covered in a nonporous material so water will not penetrate the wall.

Baluster — A vertical member or post used in a railing for stairs, balconies, and porches.

Balustrade — A railing held up by the balusters.

Baseboard — A board made of wood or composite that runs along the base of a wall that rests perpendicular to the floor.

Base molding — Type of molding used in the trimming of the upper edges of the baseboard.

Batts (Blanket insulation) — A product used to protect a house from the outside elements (cold, heat, or wind) coming into the house. Often made of fiberglass in strips of various widths and lengths to fit inside the frame of walls and ceilings. Helps to reduce energy costs by keeping heat inside the house in the winter and air conditioning from leaving the house in the warmer months.

Batten — A strip of wood used to cover or fasten the seams of adjacent boards or plywood.

Bay window — A recessed window style; it projects from the exterior wall of the house. The shape can be square or polygonal.

Beam — A horizontal and main structural member in a frame house.

Bearing (structural) wall — A main wall that supports some (or all) of the weight of a floor or the roof.

Bleeding — When resin or gum exudes from lumber. Also applied when referencing the process of extracting air or water from pipes.

Blind-nailing — Nailing so that the nail heads are not visible in the finished job. Often used for flooring or paneling.

Brace — A length of framing lumber (or a steel beam) installed at an angle to a wall that provides additional support.

Brown rot — Form of decay, in softer wood, that leaves a charred-looking brown spot. In its advanced stages, it causes cracking, collapse, crumbling, and extreme shrinkage.

Building paper — A thick tar paper or felt installed over a house's sheathing prior to applying the finished exterior roofing or siding. Used to damp-proof roofs and walls.

Casement window — A type of window that has its hinges on the vertical edge so it swings out.

Caulk — A material in a tube used to seal a seam or joint to make it smooth, waterproof, and airtight.

Cavity wall — A hollow wall formed by firmly linked masonry walls, providing an insulating air space between.

Cement mortar — A mixture of cement, sand, and stone mixed with water and used to adhere bricks, stone, blocks, and rocks.

Chair rail — A wooden molding affixed to the wall at the level of a chair back. Used to protect the wall from the chair hitting the wall.

Chalk string — A string coated in a colored chalk that is stretched between two points and snapped to make a straight line of chalk on the surface. Used in roofing and many other construction projects.

Chimney connector — The section of piping that is used to connect a stove to a chimney. Made of either metal or brick.

Circuit breaker — An electrical safety device that has a main switch that controls the electricity coming into a house.

Cistern — A tank to catch and store rainwater.

Clapboard — A board used for exterior siding, thick on bottom edge and overlapped before being nailed down.

Collar beam — A horizontal beam attached above the bottom ends of rafters to add support to the roof.

Cornice — Decorative projections above a wall or under the overhanging part of the roof to provide a finished look.

Cove lighting — Cleverly hidden light sources that direct the light on a reflecting ceiling.

Collar beam — A wooden beam no more than 2 inches thick, placed horizontally near the ridge board to support the roof.

Column — A vertical supporting member used inside or outside.

Conduction — When heat or electricity transfers through a material. Some materials transfer heat better than others. Metal is good for transferring heat, insulation is not.

Corner board — A piece of molding or trim used at the corner of a house or other structure.

Corner brace — A brace placed diagonally to support a wall.

Corian — A sturdy type of countertop made out of man-made materials.

Cove molding — Concave molding used to finish interior corners.

Crawl space — A shallow space found between the ground and the living space of a house that does not have a basement. It is used for access to pipes and ducts, and the height is not sufficient for a person to walk in the area — only to crawl around.

Cricket (or saddle) — A projection on a sloping roof used to divert water around a chimney that is in the shape of a saddle.

Crimp — A fold formed in a metal.

Cross-grain cracking — Harsh crackling of painted surfaces across the grain of the wood from the direction it was painted.

Crown molding — Cornice and interior angle molding used for decorative trim.

Dead load — The exact weight of the building materials.

Deck paint — All-weather paint usually used outdoors on a deck made of wood to protect it from the weather.

Density — The weight of an object measured in pounds per cubic foot.

Dew point — The temperature when water vapor turns into liquid.

Doorjamb — The case located on the inside of a door opening. This is where the door is attached and allows for it to open and closes. Two side jambs and one header jamb make up the case. The door is affixed to a side jamb with hinges.

Dormer windows — A window that is vertically placed and projects from a small, roof-like structure known as a dormer. These can provide architectural interest to a house and height that enables the homeowner to turn an attic into livable space.

Double-hung windows — Windows with both upper and lower sashes that move up and down. Cords and weights support them.

Downspout — A vertical channel that is part of the gutter system that allows rainwater to flow downward from the horizontal gutters placed along the roofline. They help to divert water away from the foundation of the house.

Downspout strap — Hardware used to secure the downspout to the eaves or wall of a building.

Drip cap — A piece of material or molding placed on the top of a window or door's frame to divert water away from the frame.

Dry rot — Wood rotted due to fungus that was wet at one point, causing the wood to rot, become brittle, and eventually disintegrate into powder.

Drywall (gypsum board) — Finish material used to cover interior walls and ceilings. Inner material is made of gypsum, which is in between two pieces of paper.

Ductwork — The network of pipes used to circulate warm or cool air throughout the home.

Easement — Gaining right-of-way to authorize access to an owner's land. For example, the utility company may obtain an easement in order to perform installation and maintenance on poles, electrical wires or overgrown trees. Owners may bestow easements voluntarily or, in some situations, be coerced to provide one by eminent domain. The strip of land included in the easement must be construction-free for easy access.

Eave — The lower edge of a roof that projects over the exterior walls of the house.

Edge-nailing — The physical act of hitting nails into the edge of a board.

Efflorescence — A form of salt that looks white and powdery and can develop on masonry and brick walls. It is the by-product of moisture moving through concrete and other masonry materials.

Effluent — Sewage that has undergone treatment that originated either from a septic tank or sewage treatment plant.

Exhaust fan — An electric fan that removes the stale air, odors, or heat from a room or area. Typically found in a kitchen, bathroom, attic, or workshop.

Expansion joint — A strip of fiber placed between concrete blocks, slabs, or other sections of concrete to prevent it from cracking when expansion occurs due to temperature change.

Fascia — A horizontal board attached to the ends of the roof rafters. Often used as a place to support a gutter.

Fiberboard — A board made of recycled wood or vegetable fibers and compressed into a sheet.

Fiberglass — A woven textile material made of finely spun filaments of crushed glass, rock, slag, and other inorganic materials. Often used as insulation for buildings.

Fill-type insulation — Loose material used for insulation that is placed into wall spaces either by hand or by being blown in mechanically.

Fire stop — The closure of a concealed space, used to prevent a fire. Placing 2 by 4 cross-blocking studs in the frame of a wall can accomplish this goal.

Flashing — Strips of metal used to protect the roof and other junctions on the roof (chimneys, valleys, and vents) from moisture penetration.

Floor joists — Framing pieces found on outer foundation walls and interior beams or girders.

Flue — The passageway located inside a chimney, which allows smoke, fumes, and gases to escape to the outside air.

Flue lining — A pipe made of clay that lines the inside of a chimney.

Footing — A foundation's base made out of concrete.

Foundation — The solid base built first to support the walls of a structure.

Frost line — The measurement of how far down frost has penetrated in the soil; varies around the country.

Furring strips — Used for leveling surfaces for lathing, boarding, flooring, or plastering, this is thin wood or metal attached to joists, studs, or walls. Another use is plastering or making an insulating air space, along with damp-proofing the wall.

Fuse — A short plug made with a strip of wire or metal, placed in an electric panel box and used as a safety measure. When the electrical circuit is overloaded, the metal will melt and break the circuit.

Fungicide — Chemical used to kill fungus.

Fungus — Parasitic forms of mold, mildew, and mushroom plants that live and feed on dead wood. Causes rot, mold, and decay to the wood.

Gable — The area located above the eave of a roof.

Gable dormer — Perpendicular window built out of the side of a sloping roof.

Gable end — A gable located on an end wall.

Gambrel — A roof that allows an attic to be used as a second story by sloping steeply and transforming to a shallower slope.

Gazebo — A landscape retreat that offers shelter from the shade and rain. The five-, six-, or eight-sided natural room structure has a peaked roof overhead. It can be rustic or elaborate in construction and is best placed on higher ground to view surrounding landscapes and plants.

Glazing — The act of setting glass into windows or recessed door panels.

Glazing putty — A pliable putty used around windows and in-between the glass and wooden frame.

Grade — Term used to describe the ground level around a home.

Ground fault circuit interrupter (GFCI) — Safety device that cuts the power to an outlet once it has been grounded by human contact.

Hardwood — A close-grained wood, extracted from broad-leaved trees such as oak or maple.

Headers — Double-wood planks positioned edge-wise on windows and doors to move the weight of the roof and floor to the studs.

Also: thick wood pieces serving as support to joists in a floor.

Hip roof — A roof that slopes upward on three or four sides.

Hip — The outer angle created by the conjoinment of two slopes of a roof.

Jalousies — Associated with outside shutters of wood with similar construction, these are movable windows made up of horizontal glass slats that permit ventilation and serve as a shield from rain.

Jamb — A vertical structure serving as an outline for a window or door opening.

Joist — Acting as a support for floor and ceiling loads, these are pieces of woods constructed parallel between building walls, or sitting on beams or girders.

King post — Placed vertically, this is the post found at the center-most portion of a triangular truss.

Lally column — A concrete-filled steel tube that serves as a support for girders and floor beams.

Lath — Used to create a base for applied plaster, these are numerous thin, narrow strips of wood

or metal nailed to rafters, ceiling joists, etc.

Lead — A highly toxic metal located in small segments of the Earth's crust.

Lintel — Located over windows or doors, this is a header used to support the load above openings.

Louver — Enabling air to pass through with some light but no rain or direct sunlight, this is an opening or window composed of overlapping horizontal slats.

Masonry — Building walls with materials like brick, stone, concrete or tile and bonding them together with mortar.

Molding — Often applied to wall junctures to conceal gaps, these decorative strips of material are made on a plane or curved, narrow surface. They are also used in ornamental application.

Moisture barrier — Specially treated metal or paper serving as a moisture barrier and a bar for water vapor.

Mullion — Slim framing that separates window panes or lighting.

Newel — Created by the smaller ends of steps surrounded by winding, circular staircases, this is an upright post located at the foot or secondary landing post in straight-flight staircases.

Nosing — The portion of a stair tread that is rounded and elevates above a step's riser.

Parging — Applying a thin coat of mortar or plaster over the surface of a masonry wall.

Pergola — A large and simple outdoor landscape structure with a roof, a floor made of patio materials such as gravel or mulch, and no solid walls. It offers shade and protection from the rain. It can be freestanding and a focal point to a garden, or it can be attached to the house. It is an ideal location to entertain outdoors. It has vines such as grapevines or other climbing plant materials growing over the sides and top. It can also have a canvas or cloth roof.

Pitch — The measurement term used that expresses the degree of the slope in a roof.

Plenum — A duct or chamber used as a distribution area for heated and cooled air.

Pointing — The method in masonry of filling the joints of brick and stone with mortar. This is done when either building a new wall or replacing missing mortar from an existing wall or structure. It improves appearance, and strengthens and shields the structure against weather conditions like rain and snow.

Radiant heat — Coils that radiate heat by electricity, hot water, or steam through entrenched pipes in floors, ceilings, or walls.

Rafters — Serving as a support for a roof's weight, this is a series of roof beams extending from outer walls to the center-ridge beam or board.

Reinforced concrete — Concrete supported with wire or metal bars.

Ridge pole — The longitudinal plank used to as a base to attach roof ridge rafters.

Riser — The vertical pieces of board that close the space between the treads in a stairway.

Roof sheathing — Sheets of plywood or strips of wood nailed to roof rafters to cover the roof and on which the roofing material is attached.

Sash — The portion of window frame where movable glass panes are located and set in a window or door.

Scuttle hole — A small opening permitting access to the attic, the crawl space, or the plumbing equipment.

Seepage pit — A form of sewage disposal made up of a septic tank and a connected cesspool.

Septic tank — Prior to discarding remaining waste by gravity into an underground leaching bed, this sewage-settling tank changes a portion of sewage into gas and sludge.

Shakes — Wood shingles cut manually.

Sheathing (see wall sheathing) — Before placing the finished siding or roof covering, this is the beginning cover of material located on the outer wall or roof.

Shim — Slim and tapered wood pieces acting as a leveler or tightener for a stair.

Shingles — Pieces of wood, asbestos, or other material that serve as an overlapping outer covering on walls or roofs.

Sill plate — Located on top of the foundation wall, this is the lowest component of the house frame.

Slab — About 4 inches thick, this segment of concrete is poured onto earth or gravel directly.

Soffit — The visible, horizontal underside of a roof extension or eave.

Softwood — Easily worked wood, or wood extracted from a cone-bearing tree.

Soil stack — Vertical plumbing pipe applied to the use of wastewater.

Stringer — An enclosed side of a stair, which provides support to the stair tread.

Stud — One of many strategically placed vertical boards used in framing a house that are placed at regular intervals. Used to provide support for walls.

Sub-floor — Planks of wood or plywood sheets are nailed directly to the floor joists. It acts as the first layer of flooring, and usually another finished flooring material is installed over this layer.

Sump — A pit located under the house where water collects.

Sump pump — A pump used to remove water from the sump.

Toenail — Driving nails into corners and joints at an angle.

Tongue-and-groove — The place where the protruding tongue of one board or planks fits into the groove end of another board. Boards are fit together to make a wall, floor, or decorative panel.

Trap — A bend in a water pipe to hold water and prevent gases or air from backing up into the home.

Tread — Serving as a place where people step, this is a horizontal board located on a stairway.

Truss — Structural beams arranged in triangular groups to create a firm framework and a support to span between load-bearing walls.

Valley — The intersection between two roof slopes.

Vapor barrier — Used as a shield from moisture moving through walls, ceilings, or floors, this is waterproof material such as paper, metal, or paint.

Venetian window — A window containing a single, large, preset middle pane, and smaller panes at each side.

Vent — A pipe, duct, or other type of opening used to allow air to come into and out of a house.

Wainscot — Paneling traveling from the floor to about one-third the height of a wall; it is then closed off with a chair rail or decorative molding.

Wall sheathing — Acting as the base for exterior siding, these are plywood sheets, gypsum board, or other components that are nailed to the outer face of studs.

Wallboard — Employed in a large amount of homes, this is a paper-covered sandwich of gypsum plaster that is typically used to primarily cover the wall. Also known as gypsum board, drywall, and plasterboard.

Weather stripping — Metal, wood, plastic, or other material placed alongside door and window openings to prevent air infiltration.

Weep hole (pipe) — A small hole (or pipe) cleverly placed at the bottom of the retaining wall, permitting water to seep out.

Weighted cloth — A heavy cloth joined to the end of a tool to increase weight while polishing or buffing.

Wet sanding — After joint compound has hardened in drywall finishing, wet sanding is a technique that smooths away the rough hard edges.

Wet or dry sandpaper — Whether wet or dry, this sandpaper can be put to use. For use when wet, add water or mineral oils. The glue and sand are waterproof.

White shellac — Clear shellac that has undergone bleaching.

Whitewash — Affordable, flat water paint with a lime or whiting base. This is bound loosely by glue or water-dispersible binders.

Whiting — An inert, white, crystalline pigment made up mostly of calcium carbonate.

Wood filler — When filling and coloring pores of wood, this pasty material is placed on the surface once thinned, then wiped off across the grain of wood. The material only stays in the pores as a result.

Wood finishing — The work required for producing desirable end results in sanding, staining, varnishing, and painting wooden surfaces.

Wood graining — By imitating lines found in cut lumber, this is a painting technique attempting to resemble wood grain.

Wood preservatives — Liquid chemical placed on wood to shield from decay and insect attacks.

Wood putty — Used when filling holes and other imperfections in wood, this material is dough- or paste-like and comes in many variations.

Wood stain — A translucent mix of water or alkyd-based solvent and pigment, usually in colors replicating natural wood, which permit some of the wood's natural color and grain to show through.

Work triangle — The area enclosed by the lines that join the sink, range, and refrigerator.

BIBLIOGRAPHY

Dworin, Lawrence. *Renovating and Restyling Vintage Homes.* Craftsman Book Company, California, 2004.

Heldmann, Carl. *Be Your Own Renovation Contractor.* Storey Books, North Adams, Massachusetts, 1998.

Hutchins, Nigel. *Restoring Old Houses.* Gramercy Publishing Company, New York, 1985.

Irwin, Robert. *Home Renovation Checklist.* McGraw-Hill, New York, 2003.

Litchfield, Michael W. *Renovation: Completely Revised and Updated.* Taunton Press, Newtown, Connecticut. 2005.

Maguire, Jack. *Outdoor Spaces: Landscape Design for Today's Living.* Henry Holt and Company, New York, 1987.

McGowan, John, and DuBern, Roger. *The Book of Home Restoration.* Gallery Books, New York, 1985.

Miller, Mark R., Miller, Rex, and Baker, Glenn E. *Miller's Guide to Home Remodeling.* McGraw-Hill, New York, 2005.

Nash, George. *Renovating Old Houses: Bringing New Life to Vintage Homes.* The Taunton Press, Newtown, Connecticut, 2003.

Phillips, Barty. *Home Design Guide.* SOMA Books, San Francisco, California, 1998.

Spring, Paul, ed. *This Old House: Complete Remodeling.* Sunset Books, New York, 2004.

Stephen, George. *Remodeling Old Houses without Destroying their Character.* Alfred A. Knopf, New York, 1972.

Stephen, George. *New Life for Old Houses: A Guide to Restoration and Repair.* Dover Publications, Mineola, New York, 2002.

U.S. Department of Agriculture. *Selecting and Renovating an Old House: A Complete Guide.* Dover Publications, Inc., Mineola, New York, 2000.

Vila, Bob and Howard, Hugh. *Bob Vila's Complete Guide to Remodeling Your Home.* Avon Books, Inc., New York, 1999.

Vila, Bob. *This Old House: Restoring, Rehabilitating, and Renovating an Older House.* Little Brown and Company, Boston, Massachusetts. 1980.

Web sites

American Association for State and Local History. May 2009. **www.aaslh.org/cgi-bin/statelinks.cgi**.

American National Standards Institute. May 2009. **www.ansi.org**.

American Red Cross Store. June 2009. **www.redcrossstore.org**.

American Society of Heating, Refrigerating, and Air Conditioning Engineers. June 2009. **www.ashrae.org**.

Annual Credit Report. May 2009. **www.annualcreditreport.com/cra/index.jsp**.

Bankrate, Inc. March 2009. **www.bankrate.com**.

Better Business Bureau. May 2009. **www.us.bbb.org**.

Consumer Product Safety Commission. March 2009. **www.cpsc.gov**.

Energy Star. July 2009. **www.energystar.gov**.

Environmental Protection Agency. April 2009. **www.epa.gov**.

Habitat for Humanity. April 2009. **www.habitat.org**.

The Internal Revenue Service. May 2009. **www.irs.gov**.

Let's Renovate: Home Remodeling Checklist. April 2009. **www.letsrenovate. com/checklist.html**.

Mortgage Bankers Association – Home Loan Learning Center. April 2009. **www.homeloanlearningcenter.com**.

National Association of Home Builders. May 2009. **www.nahb.org**.

National Association of Mortgage Brokers. April 2009. **www.namb.org**.

National Cancer Institute. June 2009. **www.cancer.gov**.

National Conference of State Historic Preservation Officers. May 2009. **www.ncshpo.org**.

National Register of Historic Places. April 2009. **www.nps.gov/history/nr**.

Old Houses. June 2009. **www.oldhouses.com**.

Reed Construction Data, Inc. July 2009. **www.reedconstructiondata.com**.

Underwriters Laboratories® (UL). June 2009. **www.ul.com**.

U.S. Consumer Product Safety Commission. August 2009. **www.cpsc.gov**.

U.S. Department of Agriculture's Housing & Community Facilities Program. July 2009. **www.rurdev.usda.gov/rHS/common/indiv_intro.htm**.

U.S. Department of Energy - Energy Efficiency and Renewable Energy. July 2009. **www.energysavers.gov**.

Database of State Incentives for Renewables & Efficiency. July 2009. **www.dsireusa.org**.

U.S. Department of Veteran's Affairs - Information on the Home Loan Program. April 2009. **www.homeloans.va.gov/veteran.htm**.

BIOGRAPHY

Jeanne B. Lawson

Jeanne B. Lawson has a master's degree in business administration from Simmons College School of Management and a bachelor's degree in sociology from the University of Massachusetts in Boston. She writes about business, health care, consumer topics, and technical subjects, and has worked in many phases of the business end of publishing since 1990. Since 1995, she has been repairing and renovating older homes. She has completed courses in welding, carpentry, plumbing/electrical repair, horticulture, and landscape design. Today, she continues to restore a house built in 1895 that is located in a business district that is part of the National Register of Historic Places. She has owned a landscape design business, a map publishing company, and an antique shop specializing in old books, maps, and prints.

INDEX